Leadership in Ireland

Insights from Contemporary Irish Leaders

edited by

Aoife McDermott and Patrick C. Flood

BLACKHALL
Publishing

Published by Blackhall Publishing
Lonsdale House
Avoca Avenue
Blackrock
Co. Dublin
Ireland

e-mail: info@blackhallpublishing.com
www.blackhallpublishing.com

ISBN: 978-1-84218-199-7

A catalogue record for this book is available from the British Library.

Printed in the UK by MPG Books Limited.

*Aoife McDermott would like to dedicate this book to
Mary Fagan and Kevin McDermott.*

*Patrick C. Flood would like to dedicate this book to the memory of
Barry and Noreen Flood and to his brother-in-law,
John O'Driscoll – all leaders in developing their communities.*

Aoife McDermott is a lecturer in Human Resource Management (HRM) at Dublin City University (DCU) Business School and co-director of the Health Strand of the Learning, Innovation and Knowledge (LInK) Research Centre. She completed her doctorate as a Government of Ireland research scholar and a scholar at Trinity College Dublin. Her research interests concern health service organisation and delivery, with particular interest in organisation change and people management. Together with colleagues, Aoife holds research grants from the Health Research Board and the Irish Research Council for the Humanities and Social Sciences.

Patrick C. Flood is professor of Organisational Behaviour at Dublin City University (DCU). He is head of the HRM-Organisational Psychology Group and a deputy director of the Leadership, Innovation and Knowledge (LInK) Research Centre. He is also honorary professor of Management at Northeastern University, China and academic fellow at Judge Business School, University of Cambridge. He earned his Ph.D. at the London School of Economics. Patrick teaches mainly in the area of leadership and organisational change to executives. His recent books include *Persuasive Leadership: Lessons from the Arts* (Wiley, 2010) with Stephen J. Carroll. He has worked at the London Business School, University of Limerick, Australian Graduate School of Management, Irish Management Institute, London School of Economics and the R.H. Smith Business School, University of Maryland. His teaching and research has been recognised with awards for excellence including a Fulbright fellowship. Patrick is an experienced executive educator and keynote speaker. He is a consulting editor of the *Journal of Occupational and Organizational Psychology* and is also on the editorial board of *Business Strategy Review*. He serves as examiner at Trinity College Dublin, Queen's University Belfast and Saïd Business School, University of Oxford, and has published extensively in international journals.

PREFACE

Leadership in Ireland aims to provide insight into the development and practice of effective leadership in the variety of organisations prevalent in our economy. We hope that the book will be read, and used, by practising, developing and aspiring leaders as they follow their own journeys to achieve social and organisational change.

We embarked upon the leadership interview series as we are both university teachers keenly interested in bringing the real world into our classrooms. In particular, we were seeking to bring the insights of reflective practitioners into our teaching at MBA, postgraduate and undergraduate level. However, we quickly found that there is a severe paucity of interview-based teaching materials for those who wish to bring the experience of leadership, and leadership development in particular, into their classes. We decided that we particularly wanted to hear the voices of inspirational leaders from the public and voluntary sectors, as well as the private sector. Although some previous books have provided interviews with CEOs and entrepreneurs, there are relatively few leadership interviews available for the public and voluntary sectors. These are major components of our economy, underpinning and shaping the civil society in which we live. We were curious about whether the values, motivation and dynamics of leadership were likely to be different in contexts seeking social, as well as organisational, change.

The interviews took place in a variety of contexts – from homes to offices – and were recorded by our cameraman, Daniel Fleming. The interviews typically lasted an hour and were thematically segmented. Questions were asked regarding the formative influences that had shaped each leader;

their leadership development and practice; whether they could provide examples of successful and unsuccessful innovation initiatives; their strategies for achieving change; and any advice they might offer aspiring leaders. Our video-series editor, Tom Burke, was instrumental in bringing that project to fruition. Towards the end of the video-series process, Dr Mark Rowe, one of our interviewees, suggested the development of the book at his very own book launch. We obviously took his advice! To facilitate the transition from interviews to prose, transcripts of the interviews were returned to the leaders. The leaders utilised these as the starting point to develop the chapters presented in this book. Unsurprisingly, many significantly edited the original content, clarifying points, adding examples and responding to the significant changes that occurred in our national context since the interviews took place.

We wish to thank the Learning Innovation Unit at Dublin City University (DCU) for funding which enabled the leadership interviews to take place, and the development of the associated DCU Business School leadership video series. The interviews underpinning this book were conducted between August and December 2008.

We wish to thank our colleagues for their advice and support during the development of the book, in particular Caroline McMullan, Johan Coetsee and Margaret Heffernan. We would also like to thank Kevin McDermott for his stylistic and editorial advice. In addition, Elizabeth Brennan at Blackhall Publishing was continually supportive and constructive throughout the development process.

Our greatest thanks are reserved for the leaders involved in this project. From the outset they were hugely supportive of our objectives, giving freely of their time, expertise and experience. We particularly appreciated their honesty regarding how they became leaders and their mistakes along the way, which provides particularly valuable, and rarely shared, lessons for emerging leaders. When we present the video version of these leadership interviews to our students, they are energised by what they see and hear. We are confident that, in print form, our leaders will provide insight and inspiration for the nascent and current leaders who read this book.

In recognition of the generosity of our leaders, and their willingness to facilitate and support the development of others, the royalties from this book will be given to support the work of Focus Ireland. Since being founded by Sr Stanislaus Kennedy in 1985, Focus Ireland has worked to respond to the needs of people out-of-home and those at risk of becoming homeless. The driving philosophy of the organisation is the belief that every person has a right to a place they call home. Fittingly, Focus Ireland is an organisation that has led a national quest for social justice.

A DVD documentary on leadership in Ireland, featuring the people interviewed in this book, is available. Please contact <u>nichola.osullivan@dcu.ie</u> for further details.

CONTENTS

INTRODUCTION

We live in interesting times for leadership. The demise of the Celtic Tiger has led to a more demanding business environment, in which organisations seek to right-size, retrench and reform, while maintaining day-to-day operations. In addition, the current context has created an environment where, in the absence of resources, clear public policy choices have to be made and implemented. Public sector organisations are under pressure to deliver and improve services without additional and, in many cases, with fewer resources. Public sector work practices and processes are being evaluated and reconfigured in previously unthinkable ways and the role of the social partners in public sector reform is being challenged. Recognition of the role of the social economy has increased during this time, with the work of voluntary organisations thrown into sharp relief by these developments. Voluntary organisations have quickly moved to address the ongoing and emergent social needs associated with our changed economic circumstances: providing services, maintaining communities and guiding policy development. Much prior research has emphasised private sector leadership. However, as Ireland moves to re-establish its economic position, re-evaluate its public policy and regenerate its civil society, never before has a cross-sector view on leadership been more valuable.

As the recent banking crisis testifies, the strategic leadership of organisations impacts on the economy and the population at large. Organisational leaders wield enormous power and influence in strategic decision making. Their decisions impact on the fate and fortune of organisations, shareholders and employees alike. As a result, we believe that the perspective of the upper echelons or the 'view from the top' is something that should be made much more accessible to management students – and the general public. We took this into account in our selection of leaders to interview. However, we also felt it important to interview less publicly lauded leaders. Much leadership work is quietly done, with leaders 'leading from behind' and evading the spotlight, unless to further their cause.

We do not claim the selection of leaders to have been a random, scientific selection. Indeed it is the opposite: the leaders have been selected for their personal qualities and leadership strategies. They also represent the variety of contexts in which leadership can take place. As a result, we passionately believe that the leaders represented in the book provide significant insight and guidance into the management of the diverse range of organisations prevalent across the economy.

For nascent leaders, the tangibility and 'realness' of leadership is critical to awakening the motivation to lead. The reality of leadership: the significant work behind the scenes, failed attempts at change, and the nitty gritty of decision making and working with people are often edited from success stories. So, too, are processes of 'becoming', feeding the myth that leaders are born and not made. As a result, we interviewed leaders regarding their formative experiences and underlying drivers, as well as the contextual factors which have influenced their leadership styles and practices. As change is an integral component of leadership, we also asked them about their experiences of successful and unsuccessful change processes. Hence, we adopted a three-fold focus, emphasising the *development* and *practice* of leadership and how this varied according to the *sector* and context in which the leader operates. Usefully, the leaders all provide advice to aspiring and developing leaders based on their personal experiences. Each leader represents a vast repository of experience gained in a number of different contexts, both nationally and internationally. All address their development and practice as leaders and bring their own messages, based on their individual experiences.

Our private sector interviewees include Ben Dunne, CEO of the Ben Dunne Fitness Group. His thoughtful and reflective interview is a study of resilience and leadership through focus. His 'three Ps' (Product, People and Price) provide a framework for personal and organisational success. Danuta Gray, CEO of O2, emphasises people and strategy as the core dimensions of leadership and discusses the contingencies which affect how leadership is enacted in international contexts. Niall Saul, chairman of SymbioHR Consulting and a veteran of business turnarounds, highlights the importance of creating psychological safety for those involved in change and clearing obstacles out of people's way to allow movement to occur. He also emphasises the differences in leadership during good and bad times.

In the voluntary sector we met Nickey Brennan, then president of the Gaelic Athletic Association (GAA) and former Kilkenny All-Ireland hurling winner. He draws attention to the challenges of working with volunteers and achieving leadership with a time-bounded role. Sr Stan, founder of Focus Ireland, points to the importance of listening, empowering and providing opportunities for leaders to develop. In addition, she emphasises the need for co-operation between voluntary sector organisations and the importance of such organisations moving on if the public sector or others can address a need.

In the public sector we interviewed John Lonergan, governor of Mountjoy Jail. His clarity and consistency of vision and are striking. He provides insights into the constraints on public sector leaders and emphasises that leadership does not equate with popularity. Nuala O'Loan, former police ombudsman of Northern Ireland, emphasises the importance and role of courage and emotion in leadership. She also draws attention to the systems and processes that underpin the effective functioning of organisations.

Finally, in the health sector we interviewed four individuals who provided significant insight into different approaches to achieving change in a similar context. Our health sector interviewees include Kenneth McDonald, consultant cardiologist at St Vincent's University Hospital, director of the heart failure unit at that hospital and director of the Heart Beat Trust. He adopted an enterprising approach to developing his unit, acquiring private funding and establishing a charitable trust to build and develop his service. Components of this are gradually being taken over by the Health Service Executive (HSE). He is an interesting example of entrepreneurship within the public sector. Brian Maurer, retired consultant cardiologist at St Vincent's and medical director of the Irish Heart Foundation, adopted a broader approach. He was involved in building up cardiology services in Dublin and the generation and implementation of the national cardiovascular strategy. He achieved change through policy development and engagement with existing political systems and struc-tures. Maurice Neligan, retired cardiac surgeon and journalist with the *Irish Times*, adopted yet another strategy: pushing for health service reform through service development, advocacy, critique and debate. Finally, Mark Rowe, GP and managing partner in the Rowe Creavin Medical Practice, Waterford Health Park, is an example of a healthcare entrepreneur with a social vision. His health centre is based on the concept of generative space, which aims to provide inspiring surroundings that influence individuals and the wider community.

We believe that each of these leaders has a unique story to tell about their rise to leadership positions: their vision and driving force; their values and beliefs; their methods for enrolling others in the difficult task of imple-menting strategy; and their strategies for achieving organisational and social change. Each leader has had formative experiences which have shaped their character, outlook and beliefs. Each, in their own way, is an inspirational force for change in Irish society. Each also demonstrates an altruism that is at the core of inspirational leadership in the private, public, voluntary and health sectors.

We intend for this book to provoke reflection and provide inspiration to current and aspiring leaders. In our final chapter we consider the role of emotion in leadership and the nature of leadership in tough times. We also provide an overview of the strategies utilised by the leaders to achieve change in their particular contexts.

We learnt many lessons in leadership from our conversations with these inspiring leaders. We hope that you enjoy reading the book as much as we enjoyed conducting the interviews.

1

DANUTA GRAY

CEO, Telefónica O2 Ireland

Danuta Gray is chief executive of Telefónica O2 Ireland, a position she has held since 2001. During this period Danuta has spearheaded the company's growth from a customer base of 1 million to 1.7 million – its highest ever number of customers – making Telefónica O2 Ireland the second largest mobile communications company in the Irish market. Following the acquisition of O2 by Spanish operator Telefónica in February 2006, Danuta was appointed to the Telefónica O2 Europe plc board. Danuta is the winner of the 2010 Award for Ireland's Most Trusted Leader, awarded by Great Place to Work® Institute Ireland.

With almost twenty years' experience in the mobile industry, Danuta joined Telefónica O2 Ireland from BT Europe in Germany, where she held the position of director and was responsible for managing BT's investment in Viag Interkom (now Telefónica O2 Germany). Prior to this, Danuta was general manager at BT Mobile in the UK. She has also worked abroad on assignments in the USA, Singapore and Switzerland.

She is a board member of Irish Life & Permanent plc and in August 2006 was appointed non-executive Director of Aer Lingus by then Minister for Transport Martin Cullen, TD. Danuta is also chairperson of the board of the children's charity Barretstown Gang Camp.

Danuta holds a B.Sc. in Biophysics from the University of Leeds and also has an MBA. She is married to Andrew and they have two sons.

Career Overview

I started my career as a scientist. So I did a degree in biophysics and moved into research in the pharmaceutical industry. But because it was a very solitary occupation, I decided to move to a more commercial environment. For me, it was a choice between telecommunications or information technology (IT). I chose telecommunications because there was a lot of change happening in that industry. I joined BT, via their graduate recruitment programme in 1985, just as it was being deregulated and privatised.

In BT I started off working in IT because of my background. I then moved into engineering and later made a transition into sales. I became an account manager, which effectively meant that I was a salesperson on the road. Through that process I got two or three promotions. Then the guy who had been my boss got a new job. He had given me a couple of good opportunities and I decided to go with him. As a result, I subsequently found myself in the mobile industry. There, I started off in marketing, did some customer service and eventually undertook a whole range of jobs at what might be called general management level.

After a couple of short-term assignments overseas we decided, as a family, that we would like to move abroad. We moved from the UK to Munich in Germany. Here, I took the position of director and was responsible for managing BT's investment in Viag Interkom (now Telefónica O2 Germany). It was a corporate job, rather than a hands-on and operational management role, as I was representing the shareholder in a joint venture company. My role was to liaise with the other shareholders and to get us into a position of being able to take control of the company. This experience gave me insights into a different side of the corporate world – corporate finance and law. After three years in this role I got the opportunity to interview for the job of CEO for Digifone (which later became O2) in Ireland. I moved to Ireland in 2001.

The job of CEO is a good fit for me now because it's very broad and intellectually stimulating. You are faced with challenges on a large or very small scale nearly every day. And success as a CEO is something you have to achieve through people. Thankfully, I just love seeing people succeed – and helping them to succeed. So, I would describe my job as being about people and strategy, which are the two things that I thoroughly enjoy.

What motivates you and how do you achieve balance in your life?

In terms of what motivates me – I'm quite competitive. I like competing externally, but I'm even more competitive with myself. I've always wanted to achieve the next level and set another standard to meet. I like to prove to myself that I can do things. I also like achieving through others. I get a real buzz from picking the right people, putting them in a role where they can succeed and seeing them flourish. In terms of what I am interested in at any time, I can be a bit of a butterfly. I'm always becoming interested in the next new thing and that's always driving me on to the next change or the next challenge or the next opportunity.

My continual focus on the 'next thing' has made it hard to achieve balance, in a work–life sense. What I've done over the years is learnt to box-off time. So, weekends are spent with family. I get home for tea-time on a Friday and rarely interrupt the weekend for business, if I can help it. That approach has allowed me to fully commit to whatever work challenges I have during the week. So I leave very early in the morning and tend to get home reasonably late, hopefully in time for bedtime, but obviously if I'm travelling I can't. Family–work balance works out alright most of the time. In the end, though, I think I'm like all busy people – I am the one who gets the least time. I don't often have time for myself and it's a very rare occurrence that I have a chance just to be quiet and be on my own.

What does leadership mean to you?

Whether you are in business or in public life, for me leadership is about having a vision and being able to bring people with you to achieve it. A vision is ultimately a really clear view of what you want to achieve. You have to be able to communicate it and have a real belief that it's worth doing, in order to bring people with you. Having very clear direction, the ability to communicate it and being able to bring people with you can be done in lots of different styles, but the key thing is being able to show others the path that you want them to go on. The final piece of the leadership jigsaw for me is about always paying attention to having the right people in the right job at the right time. That can change according to the times we are in and the challenges we face as a business, but it is this combination that defines leadership for me.

What has shaped you as a leader and how would those you work with describe you?

I think there's a piece of leadership which is about being authentic and being true to yourself. I am fortunate that my upbringing gave me a set of values that I strongly believe in. In addition, experience has allowed me to become comfortable with myself and to be self-aware. Being self-aware means knowing what really matters to me and being aware of my impact on others. Of course, I have learnt things from stretching myself too far and from making mistakes. Overall, I would say I've been influenced by a mix of my family and other influences – nature and nurture, I guess.

My work colleagues and others have told me that I am informal, good with people, a good communicator and creative. And they rightly say that I am always hopping on to the next new thing. Sometimes I suspect they would rather I stayed grounded in today's reality rather than moving on. I probably frustrate people who like the i's dotted and the t's crossed, because I generally want to jump to the conclusion rather than go through everything step by step.

What, in your opinion, are the characteristics of effective leaders?

In terms of my own effectiveness I'd be aware of trying not to take too much on and allowing myself to finish one thing. I also don't delegate enough sometimes, but that is because my enthusiasm or curiosity around a development or initiative can take me too far down a particular path. So, I think that every now and again it's useful to just step back and remind myself what the really critical priorities are. It's very easy to get absorbed in the melee of activity – whether it's externally or internally driven. I need to remind myself of the top two or three things that I really should be focusing my time on. So, on a Monday morning I always try to come back to people and strategy, and reassess where I am spending my time.

More broadly, I think effective leaders have the ability to be very clear in their thinking and have the capacity to articulate and communicate their vision to a wide audience. Crucially, really effective leaders do more than explain things to people. They can make things real for people. I also think that business leaders need to be comfortable with making judgement calls and to have good judgement concerning people and business decisions. Not everything is perfect and you can't analyse everything to death, so you have to make some leaps of faith. So, overall, I think the package of an effective leader contains a capacity for clear thinking, a capacity to articulate strategy and an ability to make and live with decisions, together with a sense of urgency and passion about what you're doing.

Leaders also always have to be conscious of the culture that they are operating in. I've worked in Ireland, the UK and Germany for long periods of time, as well as the US and Asia for short assignments. While the core of effective leadership is the same everywhere, the degree of formality varies across cultures. You have to be respectful of what is acceptable in different cultures and adapt your style to suit that. You can still be who you are underneath it all and the underlying traits of knowing where you're going, being able to communicate it and putting the right people in the right roles stay the same, regardless of where you work.

What do you look for in those you work with? What advice do you have for aspiring leaders?

I look for expertise or excellence that adds to the mix. I'm not looking for another me, but rather somebody who can be different. I look for people who are self-confident and comfortable with who they are. I prefer people with low ego because, with them, you get less politics. I also look for energy and passion. You have to have passion in business because it's not just a process or a methodology. Then, obviously you need the usual things around people skills. The ability to work with others and the capacity to improve the dynamics in the team are particularly important.

I would also differentiate between management and leadership. I think people have to 'jump the fence' from manager to leader. I think good managers achieve things and get things done, often using a task-driven, transactional approach. So, I would see management as a directive, task-driven role. For leaders, I would look for people with that spark of something that allows them to coach others and to create an environment where others can achieve. That's what makes the difference between a manager of tasks and a leader of people.

If I was to give advice to aspiring leaders, the one thing above all that I would say is just be yourself. People can see through you if you're not true to yourself and if you're trying to be something that you're not – even if you think you sound real. I think that's particularly important for younger people who are at an early stage in their career and who want to make an impression. It's too easy to fall into the trap of trying to be something you're not. When I was doing a sales job I had the experience of working in a really 'ladish' culture. I was the only woman on the team and it was a really aggressive, typical sales environment. For a period of time, I felt as if I had to be like them to get on and to be accepted by the team. But, actually, they could see straight through that. What made the difference was when I just relaxed into the role and was myself, as opposed to trying to be like them. I achieved more, felt more comfortable and was much more powerful and impactful as a consequence. I really believe that being yourself is critical.

This is the second piece of advice I would offer: if you get a chance to do it, do it. Take the opportunities that are presented to you. I see so many bright young people agonising over whether they should do something or not. Should they take this role? Should they move with the family? And I just think that, even if it's a disaster, you can always go back to something else. If you've never tried something, you'll never actually know whether it's your thing. So, always have a go.

Achieving innovation and improvement in organisations: what examples do you have from the front line?

Innovation for us can be technical or it can be related to an offer in the marketplace. In our industry, we can sometimes look at innovation as being a technology solution whereby we push technology into people's hands, when actually they don't need or want it. For example, in the early days of picture messaging with camera phones, the industry thought this was going to be the next big thing. Of course, in the initial stages of launch we quickly found that it wasn't the next big thing. It didn't generate the millions we had hoped for because we'd found a piece of technology that wasn't a solution waiting to happen. It took some time for that to be adopted in the marketplace.

In contrast, to provide an example of market innovation, in 2007 we were losing market share in the younger end of the market and we wanted to regain this. We made an offer in the marketplace, but it wasn't grounded enough in what really mattered to customers. We had been convinced that it was going to work. So we had to regroup over a three-month period and re-launch something different. We did a huge amount of work in really trying to understand what mattered to these customers and we crafted a new offer. We communicated in a new way with them by using a new form of advertising, a way of distributing the offer that really broke through and made a difference. It was a very simple offer on text-messaging. But it was different and it broke the mould. The essential thing was that we tried it, it worked and it was based on customer insight. So, it doesn't have to be about technology, even in our industry. It can just be about spotting an idea and letting it float.

For me, staying ahead of the competition always requires attention to customers – always. It can be too easy to jump on the bandwagon of ideas in whichever industry you are in. But, at the end of the day, we should be doing things that are based on an insight into what really matters to customers. At the moment, we're in a recession and people are worried about how much they are spending. What matters to customers is value and we have to think about what we can do to make a difference in that space. For us, this is about considering initiatives which go beyond 'better value' and actually help people to be more in control of their spend. When I reflect on our experiences, it is clear that all the really successful things we have done and which have taken us ahead of the competition are born from a piece of insight into the way customers behave and how they want to do things.

How do you bring about change in your organisation?

In my experience, change is difficult to achieve and the really important thing is to create a reason to make it happen. If there aren't external forces that are making you implement change, then you need to create a platform internally to make people sit up and recognise that there's a time and a need to change. That's very difficult, particularly if you are in a successful organisation or an industry that has always grown, because people can't understand why there is a need for change if you are or have been successful. In this situation you need to really put it into context for people and explain why, if you roll the clock forward – a year, eighteen months – the change will prove necessary or beneficial. The best thing to do is to be in control of the process. It is important to show people the value of starting change early rather than waiting until the last minute and finding that you are being forced to do things.

To achieve change, create a reason and then communicate that reason as many times as you possibly can, in as many ways as you can and to as many people as you can. Face-to-face communication is best because you can never communicate enough while going through change. It is amazing how many times you have to say something before it finally hits home. To help people understand, it's important to be able to describe things in way that's relevant and that sparks a level of engagement. Everybody wants to come to work and to do a good job. So, if you can find something, a purpose which they feel really aligned to, then you don't need to do a huge amount of persuading. In our company our focus is on being the best-loved brand in Ireland and the best place to work. Those are the two things that we always keep front-of-mind. To achieve these two things, you have to get a lot right across the business. It's important for our people to be working in the best company to work for and also the best company as recognised by our customers. We all get a buzz from that. So, if you can articulate change in the context of your key objectives, then it doesn't take a huge amount of persuasion to get people to go with you.

To achieve change, you need to create an impetus and then be very clear about what you want to achieve and the time lines in which you want to do it. Make sure you have the right set of people continuing to run the business as usual and the right set of people who are capable of making change happen.

What advice do you have for others engaged in change?

If you are undertaking change, you need to be very clear about why you are doing it. People are quite resistant to change in their own environment and you are ultimately asking people to change something, whether it's their job, the way they work or their terms and conditions. So, spell out the reason and make it clear that it's not just change for the sake of it. You also need to be clear about what life will look like at the end of the change process. If you get through that process of change, what's the objective at the end of it? What do you want to have achieved? What does success look like? Clearly lay out why you are doing it. Be able and willing to stand up and tell everyone you can, but then you also have to set a pace for the change and create momentum. You can't just spend days and days talking about the reason. You have to have a date in mind and a means by which that change is going to happen. You must have thought through your strategy in terms of implementing the change. This is because, once people understand the reason for the change, the next thing people will ask you is what it means for them. They start thinking about what the organisation is going to do and what they have to do for the change to happen. The more you can think through how you are going to get there and what people have to do, the more you can stand up and say it with conviction, and the more people will start to believe in and come around to the idea of change.

What have been your key learning experiences?

Looking back on my career to date, I probably learnt the most when I was out of my comfort zone. I could be a bit impulsive about grabbing opportunities, so if somebody asked me whether I would like to do such and such a job I'd say 'Yes', sometimes without thinking twice. Then I would land in the role and think, 'What on earth do I do now?'

The big lessons have been where I've made the biggest jumps. From the comfort of a technology background, I jumped into a sales environment when I genuinely hadn't got a clue about how to sell. That was a very fast learning curve and a brilliant learning experience. Then, jumping from sales to management was another huge learning curve, as was moving into the mobile world and taking on roles in which I had little or no experience – whether it was customer service or marketing. Finally, the biggest jumps were to Germany and then here to Ireland, and moving into corporate roles. Each one of those moves was probably a stretch just a bit too far in the initial stages. But they were the big learning experiences, and all involved making myself uncomfortable and moving out of my comfort zone.

2

MAURICE NELIGAN

Retired cardiac surgeon; co-founder of the Blackrock Clinic; health service critic; writer

Maurice Neligan is one of Ireland's most distinguished medical practitioners. He was a pioneering consultant cardiac surgeon at the Mater Hospital, Dublin from 1971 until 2006 and at Crumlin Children's Hospital from 1974 until 2002. He co-founded the Blackrock Clinic in Blackrock, Co. Dublin in 1984. In more recent years, Maurice Neligan has become a critic of the health service and an advocate of health service reform. He also writes a weekly column for the Irish Times.

Career Overview

I went to school locally here in Blackrock (Co. Dublin) and then attended University College Dublin (UCD), where I studied medicine. Once I had qualified, I perversely went on to work at the Mater. Living as I did in Booterstown, St Vincent's Hospital would have been a more obvious choice. But going to the Mater was serendipitous. It was the time when heart surgery was developing worldwide and the Mater was where it was happening in Ireland. After I became an intern, I worked there with a cardiologist and a cardiac surgeon, who were professors of medicine and surgery. I then started surgery in the Mater. I did all my exams and then stayed on to work as a junior surgeon. I began in general surgery and then moved into cardiothoracic.[1]

Later, I went overseas for training to the Queen Elizabeth Medical Centre in Birmingham. That was purely a cardiac and thoracic centre at the time. After that, I came back to the Mater during the time when the Baggot Street Hospital and Mater Hospital units were amalgamated. That amalgamation was a very good example of co-operation between doctors and examples of that can be rare enough. The Department of Health then custom built part of a cardiac unit in the Mater. There were two senior surgeons in the Mater at the time, Professor Eoin O'Malley and Mr Keith Shaw. I was there as a senior registrar and worked as the third body. I was appointed as a consultant in 1971. Then, in 1972, I became a world health fellow. I was given a sabbatical and spent the year in America, based in the Mayo Clinic.[2] After that I came back to Ireland and for thirty years I was a consultant cardiac surgeon. I worked in the Mater from 1972 and in Crumlin from 1974, until I retired.

What has motivated you in the evolution of your career and how have you achieved balance?

I had no medical relatives but became interested in medicine by reading. In particular, I was influenced by *The Story of San Michele*, which was written by the Swedish doctor Axel Munthe.[3] I was fortunate that we did have very good career guidance in Blackrock College. People talked about the various careers that were open to us. Of course, a lot of the priests would have wanted you to become a priest. But when that wasn't available as an option they talked to you about law, medicine and other careers. Interestingly enough, I subsequently found that the first-ever boarder in Blackrock College when it opened in 1862 went on to be a doctor. For me, medicine was definitely a vocation. I wanted to be a doctor. I wanted to help people. And I don't think I ever really lost that. However, it did mean that there

---

[1] Heart and lung surgery.
[2] Not-for-profit medical practice that diagnoses and treats complex illnesses.
[3] A book of memoirs, first published in 1929.

were years when having balance in my own life was a bit difficult. I tried to manage that by not becoming personally involved in the nitty-gritty of the hard-luck stories and the patient tragedies that I encountered. I had to step away from that and concentrate on the job I was doing. Also, insofar as I was able, I tried to have a balanced life on the outside. In particular, I never ever lost the habit of reading. Even to this day I would never go to bed without reading for an hour, or a half an hour. That is my quiet time.

What does leadership mean to you?

In my experience, certainly at the beginning of my career, the leader of the team was usually a professor. Then you had everybody below them. So you would look at the professor and say, 'That's the top of the pyramid', the pinnacle. And you would think, 'He's responsible for all of this.' But that didn't concern me. In fact, it's only when I actually got there myself that I began to realise how arduous that leadership role can be. That said, I'm not ever conscious of having said, 'I'm the leader of the troop.' The responsibility just arrived with the role and I did the duties that were con-sequent upon it. But I was never conscious of position or defending a position or anything like that.

In practice, my leadership style was consensus based. I tended to focus on identifying a goal to aim at and then considered how we might achieve it. Then, even if I had a sense of how to achieve something, I wouldn't go in some morning and say, 'X, Y and Z, you're doing that, that and that.' I would have been more likely to say, 'Do you think...?' or 'How do you think we can do this?', or 'How do you think we can do this better?' Occasionally I would get a nice surprise because somebody would come up with some-thing that I wouldn't have thought of myself. And when they did I had to be able and flexible enough to say, 'Good idea. We're going to do that,' and to give credit where it was due.

I think everybody has their own style, some of which I'd approve of and some of which I wouldn't. But I find that the best leaders and the best teachers are always the most understanding and the kindest. You don't really get very far by upsetting people and humiliating people. You've got to bring out the best they have – and use it.

What has shaped you as a leader?

My experience of apprenticeship and learning under other people has really shaped me as a leader. In medicine, while you can argue your corner, you are always dealing with – or should always be dealing with – people who are more experienced than you. And that is the foundation of the learning process. You aren't put on the earth knowing it all. You are relying on people to teach you, bring you along and allow you to assist and learn from them. And then they have to stand back and guide you when you are doing your first operations. Ultimately they have to sit outside reading the paper while you fly solo. And that was a ferocious responsibility that I later took on. That's the way surgeons are trained. And it has to be so.

In terms of becoming more effective in that leadership role, money would really be key. That would allow you to have the best facilities available to teach and train your staff and, consequently, the best facilities available to help your patients.

How would those who have worked with you describe you?

I genuinely don't know. I've retained pretty good relations with everybody I've worked with and trained, and with everybody I worked for and trained under. I certainly can't recall a negative relationship with a fellow surgeon in my field. There were, of course, days when you would get irritated with somebody – both when you were the boss and when you were an underling. But, beyond that, if somebody had a problem with me, I'd try and find out why; what had I done to this guy or this lady, as the case may be. But that was a very rare occurrence.

What, in your opinion, are the characteristics of effective leaders?

To be an effective leader you must, first and foremost, be absolutely comfortable in yourself. Then you must be confident in your own ability and realistic about your own ability. You must be prepared to listen and to learn, and then to say firmly, 'This is what we are tying to do folks' and 'How can we do it better?' And in such a disparate speciality as I was in, you had to go and talk to the other groupings and find out that you were in tandem, that you were all seeing things the same way. And that was often much more difficult than dealing with your own people. So, I suppose, for any leader and grouping, your inter-grouping relationships are just as important as the relationships within the group. Leaders have to manage both.

What have you looked for in those you've worked with?

For the doctors, I would have looked for compassion, humanity, loyalty and the ability to work long hours and to work hard. They must also have had a surgical skill. That can partly be learnt but an awful lot of surgeons are instinctive and born with it. Cardiac surgery is very much a team thing. It's not like general surgery, which can be much more individualistic. But any basic open heart surgery is going to require three, four or five people. It will also require integration with the nurses and the people on the heart-lung machine, and so on. They've all got to be on the same wavelength.

What advice do you have for aspiring healthcare leaders?

I would advise them to look for consensus. To talk to other people. And, more importantly, to listen to other people. However, at the same time, if they know that their goal is correct, they should push forward relentlessly. And people should not be put off by being told that there isn't public money there for whatever they want to do. There are other non-conventional ways of raising money. We did it all through the years. You shouldn't have to do that in the ideal world, but that's the way it is.

I would also differentiate between management and leadership. Leaders have an overall sense of what they want to achieve. So, you're leading and you're saying, 'This is what we're doing.' It then devolves to somebody else to manage the actual nuts and bolts of that, such as the logistics of ensuring that everybody is in place at the right time. I think the leader has to be slightly above all that. And there has to be somebody involved who will give an instruction and say, 'This is what we need here' on the day. So you need to have a good quartermaster general.

Achieving innovation and improvement: what examples do you have from the health sector?

I grew through the whole development of cardiac surgery: from the very early operations through to the coronary artery bypasses and, I suppose, more esoterically, heart transplantation. Heart transplantation was undertaken relatively late in Ireland. We waited to see what happened to the first flow of patients, after Dr Barnard's initial experience in South Africa.[4] The results from the first wave of transplantations were very unsatisfactory. They relied on giving a lot of steroids and that didn't work well. The second wave had the more up-to-date immunosuppressant drugs. And that's when we made our decision to move. We learnt from the experience of others and set out what exactly we had to do – how to build the team and where to go. And it did work for us.

What difficulties have you encountered as a leader?

I can't really tell you about any initiatives that encountered difficulties. And that's because you can't afford to set out to do something in a healthcare sense that isn't going to work too well. However, there were some experiences where it took us a long time to bring things to fruition. For example, we started to talk about lung transplantation. My colleague got involved heavily in that and it took a very long time to bring about. And it wasn't our fault. There was central foot-dragging and the usual passing the buck from Billy to Jack in the public service. Nobody was making the decisions. Eventually it did get moving, but it was a long time after it was moving in other hospitals.

How does one bring about change in hospitals and healthcare?

I think you have to establish a need. And then you have to make the need clear to the powers that be. The powers that be are political. I think that

---

[4] The first human-to-human heart transplant was performed by Dr Christiaan Barnard at Groote Schuur Hospital in South Africa on 3 December 1967. The patient, Louis Washkansky, had been diagnosed with a heart defect that would otherwise have proved fatal. Louis lived for eighteen days, but ultimately died from pneumonia. However, the operation proved that a patient could survive heart surgery.

partly explains why the health service is in difficulty right now. When they're not listening I think that, ethically, you probably have to take your requirements known to the public at large, through the media.

How have you persuaded people to support your work?

Most of the people who are or were involved in healthcare have the desire to help people. There are very few people who go into it just for the money. That means that they should, broadly speaking, be on the same wavelength. So you just have to motivate them. The best way to do that is to include people. For me, that meant asking, 'How can we do this better, guys?', 'How can we improve this?' When people are involved and their suggestions are listened to, that keeps them interested in what you are doing. And that's the key to it all. As long as they are interested in what they are doing and they are keen to help, you don't have to motivate them any further.

What advice do you have for others trying to achieve change?

Never give up. Maintain your own professional standards, your own professional ethics. Remember at all stages that you are acting for patients; and that a 'no' or a negative from administration or from politics means nothing in the larger sphere of helping people. Just keep going.

3

NICKEY BRENNAN

President of the Gaelic Athletic Association (GAA) 2006–2009;
inter-county hurler and All-Ireland medalist in 1974, 1975, 1979,
1982 and 1983; former Kilkenny hurling and football team manager

The GAA is a voluntary and amateur cultural and sporting organisation. It pro-
motes traditional Irish sports, as well as Irish culture and language. With some
800,000 members, it is the largest sporting organisation in Ireland. Nickey
Brennan was president of the GAA from 2006 to 2009. He took a three-year
sabbatical from his employer, Glanbia plc, for this period. Nickey had a long-
standing hurling career, which began with his local club, Conahy Shamrocks.
During the 1970s and 1980s, he played with the Kilkenny senior inter-county
team, winning All-Ireland medals five times. Upon retiring from playing in 1983,
he became involved in management, attaining All-Ireland success with the Kilkenny
under-21 hurlers in 1990. In 1995, he became manager of the Kilkenny senior
hurling team. He also has long-standing involvement in the administration of
the GAA. He became chairman of the Kilkenny County Board in 1991 and was
elected chairman of the Leinster Council in 2002. In 2005, he was elected president
of the GAA.

Career Overview and Evolution

I have a strong passion for the GAA. It is a very unique organisation because it has roots in every community and parish, which creates a great sense of identity. We celebrated 125 years of the GAA in 2009 and it is very inspiring when you look at what has been achieved in local parishes during that time. For me, the fact that the organisation is grounded in local communities is what inspires me to give something back.

As a player, I played hurling with my local club in Kilkenny, Conahy Shamrocks. It is a small rural club and, while we had some very good successes during my time playing for them, achieving regular success is always going to be difficult for any small club. I then moved on to St Kieran's College, which many would see as a great nursery of hurling in Kilkenny. I played with them for a number of years and had some success there. That brought me to the attention of the Kilkenny inter-county people and I played with Kilkenny at various levels from about 1970 until about 1985, when I retired.

From there, it was probably inevitable that I'd move into administration because, like a lot of people, I wanted to give something back to my club. One of my first ventures into administration was in the early seventies. I was involved in the setting up of an under-age section in the club, Bord na nÓg, as it was called. After that I took on officer roles at various levels in my own club. Later, I became involved in the Kilkenny County Board, as chairman. I then moved on to the Leinster Council and various committees in Croke Park. I eventually became president of the GAA in 2006.

How do you achieve balance?

Achieving balance in this role is very difficult. Apart from dealing with the organisation itself and aspects of policy and administration, the president has to attend functions and events to represent the GAA. At times it can be difficult to combine all of these activities. In fact, being president has almost become a 7-days-a-week job, 365 days of the year. The phone is never off and it is very difficult to get a proper work–life balance. I think you can work along with it, on the basis that it's a three-year term, but the role has grown steadily over the past few presidencies. In the future, getting the appropriate balance for the president may very well be something that the association and my successor will have to think more about.

What does leadership mean to you?

The GAA is a volunteer-based organisation and is led by volunteers, albeit with some paid administrative staff. So, the most important facet of leadership in the GAA is the ability to communicate with people. You need good trust and a clear laying out of the strategy and case for change. You also need to ensure that people meet the various targets that are set out. That approach to leadership works for the policy decisions that people will agree or disagree on. But then there are matters of a more controversial nature, where we've had to make decisions and people have been fundamentally opposed to them, irrespective of any arguments made. Clearly, where people have such strongly held views, no argument will change their perspective. So, sometimes decisions have to be made and you won't bring all of the people with you. That is a form of leadership too and it requires a very significant amount of personal strength and conviction.

When I am going into decision-making meetings, I am always well prepared. I won't go into a meeting until I am briefed on the subject matter. I think that's critical. I am also conscious that in every organisation there are always champions of various initiatives. You need to know who is going to be 'pro' the argument you're making and who will support the rationale behind it. Normally, you will have a fairly clear sense of who these people might be. It's important to have them there with you, or some of them there with you, when you make your case. And you should have your argument well worked out, in association with them. I believe that way of working is probably one of the reasons why I've been pretty successful.

My leadership style is grounded in consensus. I don't think that coming in and being dogmatic and dictatorial works, and it's certainly not a style that I have used. I listen to people, because I don't know everything about the GAA. I don't know everything about management styles and I don't profess to be overly knowledgeable on every subject. A good leader will recognise their own limitations and be happy to learn from and work with people in their organisation.

A consensus approach also fits with the strong democratic line that's inherent in the GAA. In fact, I think some would argue that the GAA is perhaps overly democratic. We have very good structures that ensure that the smallest club can, through its own members, initiate change in the association. That works well at a local level. But when you are working at a national level you must have a strong argument for change; you have to know the people you're dealing with and you have to convince them. So I would certainly be a consensus-type leader from that point of view.

What has shaped you as a leader?

I think two things have shaped me as a leader. The first is my family background. I come from a family of nine and my background is farming. My father, God rest him, had a farm and we were all expected to take responsibility and chip in. We didn't have all of the modern conveniences and automation that you find on farms today, so there was a lot more manual work. I think that gives you a certain outlook on life, whereby you link hard work with achievement. I also attended boarding school in St Kieran's College at a time when you only went home at Christmas, Easter and in the summer. You had to become a hardened individual in that context. It was a challenging life for somebody of only thirteen years of age, and I become a lot stronger in many different ways – both physically and mentally.

I was also fortunate that, on leaving St Kieran's College, I went straight to work in the Glanbia organisation, or Avonmore as it was then known. In fact, it's the only place that I have ever worked, which is quite unusual in this day and age. Throughout my 37-year career there, I've been responsible for many different initiatives. In the early stages of my career, I was given responsibility for the setting up of the whole IT section. That helped to develop my leadership skills because I was given responsibility for making it happen. I had to make decisions, I had to account for those decisions to those in authority, and I had to have a clear plan for how I was going to deliver on the objectives laid out before me. And I had to explain myself if I didn't achieve those objectives. So, from an early stage of my career, I became involved in planning, delivering on time, getting the job done well and ensuring that those who had ultimate responsibility up the chain of command were satisfied that I had delivered properly.

What do you look for in those you work with?

It is important that people have clear agendas about what they want to achieve in their role. They also need to prepare well and clearly set out their position on the subject at hand. That requires good organisation: a logical way of laying out things, and a logical way of presenting things. Following through is also very important. There are some individuals who are wonderful at developing and promoting ideas but then they don't quite follow through on implementing them. I certainly don't like that. For me, those are the important things. There are also more general standards to be maintained as well. Honesty, integrity and absolute commitment to the task are very important. Having said all of that, it is very important to emphasise that we're a volunteer-led organisation. While we can expect those standards from the employees who are paid by the organisation, you have to be conscious of when it is a volunteer who is working for you. The volunteers have a day job to do. And they're either trying to do some of their GAA work within that day job, getting a few minutes here and there, or they are doing it at home in the evening. We have become far more demanding of our volunteer officers over the last ten years.

How would those who work with you describe you?

People probably describe me as a 'hard goer', in the sense that I am some-body who tries to fit multiple activities into the day if at all possible. I would like to think that people would see me as somebody who works hard, who is pretty good at communicating, bringing people into the team, work-ing as a team player and trying to get consensus. I also hope that people would see that I always realise that we have a job to do, a decision to make and that we can't spend an infinite amount of time talking about the matter – we have to get on with it. At the end of the day, not everybody will nec-essarily agree with the conclusion we come to, but we have to get on and ensure that the job is done to the best of our ability and that we meet the targets that are set. That's the sort of individual I'd like to think most people see me as. I also think that people would recognise that I only expect of others what I can do myself, to be quite frank about it.

What, in your opinion, are the characteristics of effective leaders?

For us at senior level in the GAA, it's the ability to pull the organisation together, to set a clear direction for everyone. In general, around the different parts of the country, be it at provincial level or county level, we've been very fortunate to have people who have been strong leaders, who have managed to pull the organisation together and who have been good at helping the association to deliver a new strategy.

Indeed, we have used many of those leaders in the formulation of our most recent Strategic Plan. We also engaged with the grassroots. We got them to assess what the critical needs of the organisation were at the time, what the challenges will be going forward and how these fit into the Ireland of today, given the difficult economic environment that is now upon us.

What advice do you have for aspiring leaders?

I think that the difficult economic climate will pose challenges to leaders in the voluntary sector. I was very fortunate that my term coincided with the strong Irish economy. For the GAA, the challenge going forward is that the economic climate has changed and it means that we are not going to be able to obtain the same numbers in terms of attendances at matches and the associated income streams. So, we will have to run the association in a far tighter way.

As a result, I think the future leaders of the association are going to have to work a lot closer with people at provincial and county level. They will have to help and advise them on the whole area of proper financial management. There will be a much greater focus on budgeting and managing costs, while at the same time ensuring that the best possible service and games programme is delivered to members.

So, clearly the future officers of our association must be far more focused on the notion of planning, on the notion of setting clear and achievable targets and delivering on those targets. Centrally, we will be introducing the whole notion of merit-based funding. In other words, you will get a certain base level of funding but that will be increased if you achieve your targets. It is certainly going to be a new way of dealing with our units and we hope it will help to focus leaders' attention. In the past, when money was a lot more plentiful, there was less assessment of whether we were getting value for that money. I think that will be more deeply scrutinised in the future.

I would base one piece of advice for aspiring leaders on my personal experience. One of the lessons that stands out for me came from one particular individual who was a well-known senior executive in Irish industry. I can always recall that during debates and discussions he would sit nice and quietly and then, after ten or fifteen minutes, he would be able to encapsulate in a couple of sentences what we were trying to put together over ten or twenty minutes. He could very quickly capture what we were trying to achieve. I thought that it was a wonderful skill. It also showed the importance of actually and actively listening. I was very taken by that and it was something I felt was certainly very useful subsequently.

Achieving innovation and improvement in organisations: what examples do you have from the front line?

The innovation that stands out for me is the redevelopment of Croke Park.[1] The project initially started out as the development of one side of the ground. That was received very enthusiastically, with a lot of support from within the GAA and from the corporate sector. The fact that the development of that side went well meant that the GAA grew in confidence and began to consider the wider development of Croke Park. The process was eventually completed with the development of what we call the Northern End (or Dineen Hill 16) of Croke Park. That redevelopment took place at a time when, from an economic point of view, it was questionable as to whether the GAA could undertake such a large-scale and costly development. It did entail a bold step by the GAA, particularly because there was no guarantee of government funding – although that did come subsequently. But, nevertheless, the majority of the funding had to come from and be found within our association. Many doubted that we had the capacity or support to do that. So what we achieved was fantastic and I think the GAA was rightly lauded for its go-ahead and innovative approach to that development. Croke Park is now recognised as one of the greatest

---

[1] 1993–2005.

sporting venues in the world and has received a new audience during the last three years because of the rugby and soccer internationals.

A more recent example of innovation is that, during 2008, we undertook a complete re-branding of the GAA. In the past, people would have wondered what relevance branding has for the GAA. However, given the scale of the organisation and its indelible link to communities everywhere, I was of the view that our image and our brand looked a bit stale. It hadn't been reviewed for a long period of time. So we engaged a company to assist us in that regard. But, rather than bring them in and let them come up with what should be our new brand and our new image, we engaged with over eight thousand people around the country. We listened to what people from the grassroots and all walks of life had to say to us. Indeed, we conducted a similar exercise in drawing up our Strategic Plan. And people were not slow to tell us about the association. I must admit that the one thing that will always stay with me is how positive they were. They did, of course, have some things to say about us that perhaps we didn't like to hear, but it is important that all views are sought and listened to when one is looking at such a major review.

Our new brand image is now being rolled out around the country. I think it shows that the association has really arrived into this new century and is vibrant and strong. You see the new image of the GAA presented differently on all sorts of merchandise.

I suppose the final example of innovation, and I know there are many more, was the sponsorship of our championships. These have been completely reviewed and revamped. In the past, our two main competitions had a single sponsor, and this sponsor was the main brand associated with the competitions. We have now moved to a multi-sponsor model. To do this properly, we decided to bring the management of the sponsorship in-house. So our championships are now branded as the GAA Championship, in association with the various sponsors. We undertook this project at a time when the economic challenges weren't as obvious. But we managed to achieve our objective in that regard. We now have six major sponsors on board across our two main championships, three with each. This marked the GAA's new approach to dealing with the corporate sector. Perhaps in the past we were seen as an organisation that took from the corporate sector but didn't engage or develop the relationship with them as much as we should have. We now see ourselves as working in a real partnership model, whereby those who are on board with us and invest in us expect and receive deliverables from the GAA in order to achieve their business objectives.

What, in your opinion, are key success factors in the voluntary sector?

Unlike business in the true sense of the word, we're a not-for-profit organisation. However, that is not to say that the bottom line is unimportant. We are an organisation that currently delivers about 80 per cent of what we take in back to our units. So, out of every euro that comes into Croke Park, we're delivering 80 cents of that back. That happens through grants for infrastructural developments, coaching and development initiatives, or the employment of people at various levels, be they administrators or coaching personnel. The other 20 per cent is used to run the organisation, which includes administration and running our games. So we have to deliver a quality bottom line to run and develop the organisation. At the same time, it's a challenge to grow the resources that we take into the organisation year on year. So, while it is not about making profit, we are concerned with generating as much funds as possible to disperse down to the grassroots of the organisation. At the end of the day, we can only distribute and deliver what we get in.

The other major challenge for us is the delivery of the Strategic Plan, which sets out targets until 2015. The targets are deliverable over three time frames, over 2009, 2011 and 2015. Within the Strategic Plan, we have identified a broad range of issues that need to be addressed. The issues are games-related, play-related and also deal with the challenges associated with the urbanisation and ruralisation of Ireland. They are to do with player welfare, finance, governance and with infrastructural development. And that is just a snapshot of the issues involved. But the key thing is that we now have very clear and measurable targets in place. These provide us with a template to measure the success of our organisation. Our big challenge is to ensure that our staff and volunteers at various levels meet those targets. And I think, probably for the first time ever, in relation to many of our activities, we have begun to sit down to set goals and targets with our counties. They now know what is expected of them. It shouldn't, therefore, be a particular surprise to them at the end of the year to discover whether they have achieved those targets. Obviously, the funding to them will be partly based on their achieving those targets.

What have been your key learning experiences?

I learnt a lot from the process that led to the temporary relaxation of Rule 42, which allowed rugby and soccer to be played in Croke Park. Over the years, there had been various unsuccessful attempts from different counties to relax or get rid of that rule. During the process, there was a lot of emotion on both sides. It probably eventually came about because of the fact that the motion was for a temporary relaxation, for the period of the redevelopment of Lansdowne Road. But the GAA went through a very difficult time. The motion was rejected on a number of occasions. There was a lot of animosity and ill will in the association from people who held very strong but differing views on the matter. It was passed in 2005 with a very strong endorsement. In fact, over 75 per cent were in favour. That strong majority was exactly what the association needed. It certainly didn't need a close call on the matter, to be quite frank about it, because the issue could have become very divisive then. Really, what that process showed me was that we can develop very strong and emotive arguments on many subjects. But the key thing is that when you go back for a second run at something, you can't go back with the same argument. And it can often take a couple of shots at something to get proposals moving forward.

How do you bring about change in your organisation?

There's a couple of ways to achieve change. First of all, the GAA lives in the real world and we have to keep in step with the rest of the country. So, there are forces outside of the GAA that determine change. For example, government strategy over the last number of years has affected us. The Government's spatial strategy has probably had some adverse effects for the GAA through its influence on the development of rural towns and cities. The GAA would, at its heart, have always been seen as a country or rural organisation. But people who previously would have lived in the country now have to move into towns and cities to get houses, because building in the countryside has been increasingly limited. That means that our members, who would previously have happily built on their parents' land or bought a site, have to come into the city. And, while they themselves may continue to play with their home club, their children who are born in the city will tend to gravitate towards the local city club. The association therefore faces the challenge of whether there are enough clubs in these urban areas to accommodate them. And whether there is land to develop more pitches. And land has been exorbitantly expensive over the last number of years.

You have the opposite problem in rural areas where there is less of a population and fewer people available to play on teams. The GAA has recognised that as a problem and it is specifically identified within our Strategic Plan as something that we have to face up to right now. We're engaging with the Government and local authorities to meet some of the challenges that have arisen relating to both of these situations. They recognise that we're not just about delivering games to those young people. We're delivering a social, cultural and sporting outlet to them. That is important in terms of their physical, mental and social development. Health issues can also be alleviated to some degree by the provision of sporting facilities. And the GAA is at the heart of helping to deliver those sporting facilities.

So, change can come from outside the organisation, but more usually it tends to come from within. We have many groups within our association that handle various aspects of our business. Change often emerges from their work. For example, it might come from a group dealing with infrastructure, it could be a group dealing with the developing area of interculturalism in the country, or dealing with coaching and games development. We have sub-committees dealing with key issues, in line with policy. And these committees generally work at both provincial and county level, developing and selling ideas and making sure that they are brought up to the top level and become policy in the association. So, achieving change is about engagement; it's about thinking through your strategy and it's about selling it as well. And, finally, it is about backing it up with appropriate systems and finance to ensure that it can be delivered.

Do you think lessons can be drawn from sport for business and vice versa?

Irrespective of what sport you're playing, two key ingredients that make you successful are teamwork and strong leadership. Strong leadership requires the leader to be effective at communicating their message. This can be best illustrated by successful team managers, particularly when they are talking tactics to their players to motivate them. When players have absolute belief in what their manager is saying – that brings out the best in them.

I think the GAA can learn from business. In particular, we can get better at the whole issue of managing our finances and improving our governance structures. We have the same challenges that most businesses face, but we are less developed in terms of dealing with them. In the past two years, I set up a national audit committee and they have identified a number of key areas for action in the association. We are already working on those and on compliance with the appropriate standards. But again, because we are a voluntary organisation, that is a challenge, because expecting the same standards and disciplines to apply to volunteers can be difficult. Nevertheless, given the scale of the organisation and the activities that take place, it is very important that people in the GAA understand the notion of compliance and responsibility. We have a responsibility as an organisation to educate people in these areas and to bring in outside expertise for areas in which we are lacking. We want to help people undertake their business in a more open and transparent manner. We are getting better at it. There is no doubt about that. But we have some way to go yet.

4

NIALL SAUL

Chairman, SymbioHR Solutions; formerly director of human resources (HR) and organisation development (OD) at McNamara Construction; former group head of HR and OD at Irish Life & Permanent plc; former group head of HR and OD at Waterford Crystal Worldwide

At the end of September 2009, sometime after completion of this chapter, Niall Saul left his role as HR director at McNamara Construction, a position he held since February 2007, to take up the role of executive chairman of SymbioHR Solutions, a company of which he is a part owner with two other colleagues. Symbio is a consultancy practice specialising in organisational change, restructuring and development, and the provision of a range of HR-related support services. Prior to 2007, Niall was group head of HR and OD with the Irish Life & Permanent Group, which he joined in July 1997 from Waterford Crystal, where he was HR Director. He has worked as HR/OD director at CPI Holdings, now the Grafton Group, and Packard Electric, a subsidiary of General Motors.

Niall has over thirty years' experience in the areas of HR management, OD, industrial relations, change management, and merger and acquisition projects. He has worked in consultancy posts in the industrial relations area with the Irish Business and Employers Confederation (IBEC) and the Irish Productivity Centre

(IPC). His particular areas of interest are the role of HR in turnaround or survival situations, the management of change, the creation of competitively focused organisations, and the development of competence-based approaches to performance management.

Niall holds a master's degree in Change Management and is a non-executive director of a number of organisations. He is a fellow of the Chartered Institute of Personnel Development (CIPD), former chairman of the HR and Social Policy Committee of IBEC, an adjunct professor of the National College of Ireland (NUI) and a visiting lecturer on master's degree programmes across a number of Irish universities.

Career Overview and Evolution

When I left school I joined the B&I Line shipping company. The company was being nationalised at that time and a lot of young people were recruited. I became involved in the union side of things. I ended up as chairman of the union section within a year of joining the company. It was quite interesting and I got involved in all kinds of participatory initiatives that were taking place at a time of major change for the shipping industry.

Later, after four years in B&I Line, I left and moved to the other side of the table. When you're on the union side, you're negotiating with people and you often think, 'I can't see why they can't see the solution to this issue because it's so easy.' I thought that when I got over to the other side I could find those answers. It's not quite as simple as that in practice, but that was how I decided to make the transition to the management side of industrial relations. I liked that a lot.

From there, I moved into more strategic areas involving restructuring organisations, dealing with turnarounds and looking after organisation capabilities. My career has developed from there and I have spent most of the last thirty years restructuring companies. These have mostly been organisations that have had very good track records and have fallen into crisis. Turning them around has really been my main career focus. And I can honestly say that I haven't had a boring day in the last thirty-five years. Over that period, I have been privileged to be actively involved in designing, leading and supporting major change and restructuring programmes in a wide range of industries, including the banking/financial services,

European automotive, construction, retail and electronics industries, in national and international environments. I have had some great opportunities to develop and bring to life the role of the HR function as a genuine partner in these businesses and in making major change a reality.

I came to McNamara Construction in 2007. At that point, the construction industry was flying. The view was that there was a need for professionalisation in the management capability of the construction industry. The industry has tended to focus on professional skills and has been relatively underdeveloped in terms of professional management. It's generally been a business that's been driven primarily by individual ownership rather than broad-based team or process-based management. About three years ago, Bernard McNamara, the then chairman of the group, felt that there was a need to look at professionalising management to achieve more measurability and predictability in the organisation's processess. The aim was to take the managerial group that was already in the company through a process of professionalisation. Improving their skill-set was to facilitate their growing the business by developing innovation. The organisation would have a good name for innovation in the industry, but for my two and a half years in that role I was working to develop that. That was the brief really.

At the same time, McNamara was working on a major change programme, designed to move to a much more systematic approach to how projects are run. To achieve this, Bernard brought in a guy named John McGowan and myself. John had a strong record of achievement, running the Intel plant in Leixlip and latterly heading up all construction for Intel worldwide. In addition, I came in on the organisation development side. Clearly, from the outset of that project, we had to adapt to cope with the big down-turn in the market...and in that situation my own previous experience in restructuring and rightsizing came into play.

What drives you?

I have an interest in doing a good job and making a contribution to changing things and making things a bit different. In particular, I have an interest in organisations that have the fundamentals and potential to succeed but may have fallen into tough situations. In many cases, particularly in some traditional organisations that I have been involved with, they have in the past gone through periods of marked success. However, they have, for a variety of reasons, failed to cope with changing market circumstances and slipped over time into real crisis. Indeed, in looking across the range of organisations I have worked with, in many different industries, I have been surprised by the marked similarities in their histories and the patterns that they have in common.

Generally, most people in organisations want them to be successful. It sometimes frustrates me that organisations don't manage to tap into that. They tend to miss the fact that a lot of people come into work to do a good job. And sometimes the processes that exist in organisations prevent them from doing that. People are quite prepared to listen to hard messages and make quite big changes if they have a context in which to do it. So, I get satisfaction from doing that, even if you have to go through tough situations to get there. If you look at most successful change programmes, it's been the main role of top management to create the vision and then clear the barriers out of people's way and let them get on with doing the work. Seeing that happen and turning around organisations from having little hope to being profitable does give me quite a buzz.

My role in McNamara has been different. McNamara was the first company I came into that was flying. I came in with a focus on training and development. But, actually, in the last eighteen months in the role I found myself using the skills I have acquired in the past, because the construction industry generally has fallen into a crisis. Although the fall in housing was expected, the credit crunch has had a huge effect on the larger construction companies. Development and construction activity has dropped dramatically due to the emergence of a vicious circle of credit drying up, falling property values and high labour costs in the industry relative to the productivity delivered.

In the construction industry, the key challenge for leaders is to manage what has been a very labour intensive and relatively unstructured production process. If you look at current best practice in construction, you're looking at a move towards the use of technology because labour costs in the sector are very high and productivity isn't matching that cost profile. So, unless there is a significant increase in labour productivity, by increasing quality output that requires no rework at the current prices, then new technology and ways of building will continue to be developed and used. This is particularly the case as prices available for projects in the market continue to fall. The more you can use technology to bridge that gap, the better.

A lot of the disciplines that apply in multinational businesses are now being applied to contracts of construction – and leadership is required for this process. People used to say that you can't compare two building sites with each other. But, actually, if you start to look at the metrics behind construction, they're no different to those used by Dell or Vodafone. People in the industry are learning that, particularly as they move to compete in the EU. For example, a lot of the civil engineering work is now being quoted for by Portuguese and Spanish construction companies. One construction company from Portugal has built five hundred kilometres of motorway in the past three years. This country hasn't built five hundred kilometres of motorway in the last three years – or in the last ten years, in fact. So there is a different level of business experience evident internationally. And we are going to have to compete with them in the future. The EU is their market as far as they are concerned. Also, as our own home market is facing difficulty, we must look to see what elements of the construction and professional capabilities we have that can be exported. The Enterprise Ireland Leadership 4 Growth programme, in co-operation with Duke Corporate Education,[1] is a major driver in this.

How do you achieve balance?

I never get too emotionally involved with the issues I'm dealing with. For example, I had a situation in Packard Electric some years ago, where we were going through a fairly major change. We finished up negotiations at about four o' clock in the morning in the Labour Court and I went home and went to bed. A lot of people couldn't understand how I could go home and sleep because there was such a critical vote to be held by the unions on our final proposals for the future of the business. If the deal from us on the table was rejected, the plant would close and over a thousand jobs

---

[1] An international learning and development company that helps organisations achieve their goals.

would be lost. In the end, out of a thousand people they only voted by a majority of eleven to keep the plant open. But, you know, you have to just say, 'Well, look, we've done what could be done to get a workable agreement and we'll see what happens.' I think that's really it. I am of the view that you can only do what you can do and I tend to stay a bit detached from the emotions of it. So, I have a healthy sense of not taking myself or my role too seriously. I tend to be capable of detaching from situations reasonably well. I have an interest in things like sport, which allow you to vent your frustrations in other ways. Really, that's it; I think that balance is achieved by being able to step back from any situation and being able to distance yourself from the kind of emotion that drives people into stressful positions.

What does leadership mean to you?

Movement is the word I always associate with leadership. It's about moving an entity from one situation to another. That involves identifying the agenda, being reasonably sure that it's the right way to go and then convincing other people to join it. It's quite a political thing rather than management as such. I see management as being more at the control side and more about the process piece, but the leadership piece is about moving people's attitudes and mindsets. That involves helping to build a bridge that people feel they can cross. I often use a river analogy to explain this. There are some leaders who sit on one side of a river bank and say to people on the far side that 'the answer is over here, stupid' and then wonder why people resist or refuse to move. I think real leaders stand on the same side of the bank and help people build bridges that they can actually walk across. For most people, change is something that they fear unless they feel they can have some relevance in the changed environment. Really, for leaders, it's a question of contextualising the change in that way so that as many people as possible – at least a majority – can see that if they are prepared to go the journey that they will have relevance in the new set-up. To me, that's the core of leadership: being able to tap into the fact that most people come into work wanting to do a good job and to give them a context in which they can do that.

My own leadership style is fairly relaxed, in the sense that I tend to keep a fair number of options open for a period of time, to allow a reasonable amount of discussion. I'm prepared to listen to people. However, once I decide on a direction then I probably get more direct and rigid. So, it's probably a consultative kind of leadership that can become fairly directive at the crunch point – once I feel a tipping point has been reached and the focus must move from thinking to getting something done. I also have a capacity to absorb and contain other people's anxiety. That's probably a thing that people value in change programmes. Particularly if you're the main leader of an organisation, it is useful to have someone like me with you who can share some of the burden. In my role, I've never been a CEO in an organisation, but I've always worked with the actual formal leader. My role has sometimes been to contain their anxiety about the size of the challenge and convince them that they can actually do it. At times that main leadership position can be a very lonely place to be for the person concerned – and I try to be as supportive as possible in those situations.

What has shaped you as a leader?

As I mentioned, I have a pretty fundamental belief that when people come to work they want to do a good job. I think that the real test for leaders is to get into people's heads and understand and help them. I see the role of top leadership as removing the barriers from people performing because, in my experience, very few people come into work to pass the time of day. So, leaders need to find out what it is about the organisation that is stopping people from engaging. People like to be involved with something that is successful and tapping into that is my biggest interest.

I think the other key thing is to be pretty direct about the issues. You need to show people the reality and establish it as fact. Then you need to show what people must do. And be honest that, if they do these things, the situation will be better for some people, but maybe others won't be able to stay, or whatever. People like clarity. They tend to deal with that better than with the uncertainty of not knowing one way or the other. In Ireland in particular, you can see a number of organisations that limp from one crisis to another. And, really, that's often been because the organisation has stopped short of the full truth. They accept a partial solution, so the things come back and hit them again because the core issues have not been addressed.

For these two reasons I have a preference for communicating directly with employees on the change agenda. I also work within the organisation to create the concept of an informed and questioning workforce through direct and regular communication sessions. These sessions try to ensure that people at all levels in the company know the threats and opportunities facing the business, the drivers of value and the context in which those drivers must be utilised to deliver value. I do not believe in abrogating that responsibility for ensuring clear communication of the core issues to the trade unions or representative bodies. Those bodies do have their place and a representative role, but communication and leadership of the company is not their responsibility. It is the responsibility of the top management.

How would those you work with describe you?

I think that they would describe me as being constructive, reasonably helpful, fair minded and honest. I would tend to give people a fair amount of scope in terms of doing things. I think they would sometimes say that I allow too much scope in the sense that they would probably prefer more boundaries and structure than I give them. Sometimes, in 360-degree feedback, people have said that I give them quite an amount of autonomy but they would prefer if it was more tightly managed. I also think they would be concerned that, at times, I tend to leave decisions open until I feel the time to move from thinking about the issues to taking action has been reached....and my idea of when that tipping point has been reached may sometimes be later than others are comfortable with. That can cause some anxiety, but I do have a good level of confidence in my ability to get that timing correct, although that is not to say that I have always been 100 per cent right in that over the years. Once we decide on a particular route, I think that people would say that I become very focused and probably a bit directive and demanding. But generally they would see me as a fair-minded and constructive person.

What, in your opinion, are the characteristics of effective leaders?

Effective leaders have a clear vision about where they want to go. They are able to articulate that to get people to buy into it. Most importantly, they can understand the concerns that people have and are able to deal with the valid ones. In describing this, I use the term 'contextualisation' a lot. For most people, if you can contextualise the need for change for them, that's the start of the process. Then you deal with what they actually have to do and what's in it for them.

When I think of what would have made me more effective in the past, sometimes I wonder about the timing of some interventions; whether, if I had had a deeper understanding of some things, I could have chosen better timing. Also, sometimes people think that my capacity for emotional containment can create uncertainty in people. Sometimes that is because they are quite anxious and they are concerned as to why I'm not that anxious. Generally speaking though, over a wide range of situations in a large number of significantly varied organisations, I think the record shows that my analysis and judgement on the dynamics of change processes stand up well to critical scrutiny.

What is the role of a leader in good and bad times?

Strangely, I think the leadership agenda when times are good is much harder. You have to convince people who have been and often still are quite successful that the way they're doing things isn't the best and will cause serious problems if it continues unchanged. People often look at you and say, 'Well, why do we need to make the change? We're doing fine.' Indeed, it is often this 'blindness of the successful' that leads some organisations that have been very successful to fall into crisis and sometimes total failure. They may be unable to identify the changes in their marketplace and may face resistance to making the necessary changes from sometimes very senior managers and directors. Often, change may involve dismantling what senior managers have spent years building. The real issue is to get people to think about what we are going to be facing in the future.

In a crisis situation, it's actually easier to get people to engage. When you have a burning platform, you don't have such a range of choices and it's easier to encapsulate what needs to be done and get it across clearly. People are feeling the heat and they too are looking for solutions.

If you look at a lot of organisations that have gone through crisis, what you will see is that they have been very successful organisations at particular points in time. One of the big problems in organisations is that the leaders often struggle to bring themselves to undo what they have built – which is what you have to do to survive. Therefore, you do see a lot of change processes where a number of the people on the top team of quite successful organisations aren't there at the end of the change or restructuring process, because it's too much for them to dismantle what they had built.

What do you think are the challenges of international leadership?

In undertaking leadership internationally, I think the most important thing is to get an understanding of the culture that you're operating in. I had an experience as a minor partner in a joint venture with a Belgian bank. They moved into Hungary with a partnership approach. That was probably the wrong style for Hungary at that time, for a people who had just come from the command-and-control style of a communist system. The jump to a more democratically based model was seriously countercultural, and people in the organisation struggled to adapt. In contrast, General Electric (GE) came in and bought another branch-based retail bank in the same market and took a very command-and-control view of the world. Twelve guys from GE came in and said, 'We're the management' and actually the system adapted itself better to that because it was closer to what the people in the organisation had been used to...an old command-and-control system rather than one based on partnership and collaboration. Culturally, at that time the GE approach was a better fit. It was also interesting to see that, in Hungary, people didn't value themselves on the basis of their role, but on their level of educational achievement. Within the system, educational achievement had become the currency for establishing a measure of value and a tool of career management.

What do you look for in those you work with and in appointing people to leadership roles?

The biggest quality that I look for is enthusiasm. Sometimes I would look for that over direct intellectual capability (assuming the minimum intellectual capability required to do the job competently is there) because I think that you can work quite well with somebody who is enthusiastic and willing to learn. By creating the right culture in a team, you can make up for each person's shortcomings within a group and make the collective capability of that group much stronger than the sum of its parts and less dependent on the unique capability of any single individual. Also, I like people to be ambitious. Not in a self-centred way. But to have an ambition to deliver what the team or the business wants or needs done, and to do so to a standard higher than is expected. Most people who have worked with me have done fairly well afterwards, so that's probably an indication of how it works.

In appointing people to leadership roles, I look for the capacity to take a wider view, the ability to contextualise what they need to do and to get people to come on side with them. So it's the ability to engage with people. The technical stuff is just technical stuff, but the real thing is about getting the organisation to move forward. Mostly that is achieved through engaging people at all levels of the organisation.

What is involved in coaching and developing leaders?

One of the big things in coaching leaders is to try to get people to look outside their functional specialism and get them to understand what general management means. That entails getting them to understand what it means to be functioning in a team and having to see things through the eyes of other people with different skills, values and perspectives. So, for me, it's a question of trying to identify a gap between where a person is and where they need to get to in terms of making a contribution, and for them to understand why they need to go up to that level. I like to focus on conversations around agreeing the core competencies required to be effective in the role the person has at present. Then I try to get a shared agreement on how they score on those competencies and from there see what areas, if worked on, would deliver most for them in terms of realising their full potential in that job and their wider career.

I think the main roles of a good coach are to be an empathetic and trusted companion in the development process. They need to be a serious-minded challenger and a professional resource for the person being coached. But the coaching process needs to be owned by the person being coached, and they must carry the primary responsibility themselves for engaging with the process to the level necessary to deliver the success they require. The core of the coaching process is the generation of constructive, challenging, adult discussions.

What advice do you have for aspiring leaders?

I remember getting advice when I was leaving B&I. The HR guy at the time said that the one thing in this area is never to be tempted to lie for expedience because it always comes back to bite you. That's probably the one thing that has stuck in my mind in the last thirty years. Trust is a critical issue in the area of change and restructuring. I actually find that there is no need to be dishonest. People appreciate it if you are upfront and, in most change processes, people prefer to know what the issues are, no matter how tough. Even if it means that people have to go through a downsizing programme, they prefer to know. Also, if you become seen as being a straight-talking person to deal with, people put a huge value on that and you can find that people gravitate towards you and are inclined to place significant trust in you, even in times or situations that may be organisationally or personally difficult for them.

Another thing I think is almost sacrosanct within any change programme is that whatever number of jobs you have to downsize stays fixed and isn't negotiable. Once you do that, people will then come to know that what you're saying is true, whereas, if you make the number of people that have to go flexible, it means that you haven't been respectful enough to actually do your planning right. I think that damages your credibility.

Finally, you should surround yourself with people who are constructive in their viewpoint but questioning in their approach. And you should try to create a culture of shared ambition, genuine engagement, mutual support and challenge in any group you are either leading or participating in within any organisation.

Achieving innovation and improvement in organisations: what examples do you have from the front line?

One set of innovations in the construction sector emerged to deal with the cost of blocklaying. There has always been a tradition of blocklayers in

Ireland, but the cost of blocklaying simply went off the affordability scale during the boom due to restrictions within the craft and an insufficient number of trained craftspeople. If you compare Ireland to Holland, which has similar characteristics to us – particularly high labour costs – you can see that the Dutch deal with that by using a lot more technology in building. In Ireland, what has happened is that new techniques have been brought in, which use a lot of glass and other materials that require less blockwork. I expect that, over time, blocklaying will either revert to more affordable levels or slowly fade from sight as new buildings are constructed using different and more cost-effective but equally aesthetic processes.

In terms of other innovations, the problem is that, in the Middle East and Far East, large floors of office buildings are being constructed seven or eight times faster than what we can do here. They use different mixtures of technology to do that, notwithstanding the relatively low labour rates, and the question for us is whether we have the ambition and capacity to reach those standards. In turn, that may enable our construction sector to develop a meaningful and competitive export capability.

What do you see as being key to staying ahead of your competitors?

In the construction industry, it's about the construction of a building that is more acceptable to the customer. If they are spending eighty or ninety million on a building and you ask them what they would like to get, what they are looking for is to overcome or eliminate unpredictability of price, quality, functionality and completion dates. They are not necessarily looking for the cheapest building, but the one that performs predictably. If you think about that, those requirements have driven change in a lot of industries.

The really successful companies in the future will have a line of transparency with the customer, so that customers can see exactly what they are buying. It's a quality thing. McNamara have been working on a quality initiative called the McNamara Way, which is all about building in predictability and uniformity. One benefit of this initiative is that it will allow the movement of managers and engineers from one site to another, with uniformity of system. Historically, in the construction industry in general, sometimes the record keeping depended on the site manager and their particular quirks rather than a standard approach. So, they are the main areas where you will see changes, as approaches like the McNamara Way bring those levels of transparency and predictability to the client. The capacity to win a project will depend more on the provision of that concept of delivering real value.

For construction companies, the other major choice will be whether to stay focused on Ireland or to develop the capability to compete on a wider scale. Clearly over the next couple of years construction is going to become a much smaller industry in Ireland than it has been in the past. The question is whether we put together some of the experiences we had in the good times and employ them elsewhere. I don't think that we will be sending blocklayers and carpenters to places like Abu Dhabi or Qatar, as the labour market is cheap there. But we could use our project managers, construction managers, engineers and quantity surveyors to provide the management cohort for particular projects. There is also potential for Irish professionals to have a role in design and project consultancy. So, really, our current challenge is to see how the business can use its capability – for which there is not going to be a great need in this market for the next two or three years – to compete elsewhere.

How can organisations identify ways to shift their capabilities?

As I have said, it's important to look outside the country. Something else that we have done is to engage with Enterprise Ireland. They ran a programme for the software industry whereby they got thirty leaders of software companies to look at globalisation. They are in their second tranche now. We have done some work with them on developing a similar programme for the construction industry, covering architects, design engineers, professional practice, material providers and construction people.

The first programme has now been delivered, and already some of the participants, including McNamara, have made progress in export markets. It is starting to get people to think about how you would globalise or internationalise the Irish construction business. Clearly there is a lot of work out there, particularly in parts of the Emirates at the moment. I became involved with Enterprise Ireland on the design aspects and helped to pick providers for the programme. I am pretty confident that it will actually take the industry to a different level. The second programme is due to start in early 2010 and has been widened to include environmental and 'green technology' companies.

Over the next four or five years, we will have three cohorts through that programme. Having ninety leaders of construction in Ireland skilled up to a particular level and ability will change the way we think about things and particularly the capability of businesses. If you project ten years out, that kind of initiative will have a significant impact and really could make a big difference to the country.

I think the other option is to look at the whole energy and green agenda. In some of the work being done by FÁS, despite its other much publicised problems, a range of young, well qualified craftspeople have been sent to California. California is a leading edge centre for green thinking and energy efficiency. Initiatives such as this act as seed capital, generating the possibility of new green enterprises in our economy. Those people will be coming back to the Irish system over time and setting up small companies. So, there is a lot of potential out there. The worst thing we can do is sit and feel sorry for ourselves because the market at home has slipped from its former high level of activity.

How do you achieve change within your own organisation?

I think that to achieve change you need to get the organisation to have a shared view of what the threats and opportunities to it are. This is pretty standard stuff, in most companies, but it is important to get the balance between analysis and action right. For example, this is the first time in fifteen years that people in the construction industry will have to be concerned about whether there is going to be a project to start on when the current one finishes. People in the construction industry are practical. They tend to sit down and say, 'Let's find a solution.' I suppose my task was to get them to do a bit more thinking before they picked a solution. There are organisations who have rushed out to the Middle East without having really considered who they are going to work with and what way they are going to work. Picking the wrong answer to those questions can lead to really serious problems. So, understanding the market you are going into and the dynamics of it does require thought. We are now finding that people are starting to think about that. We have a couple of guys who worked in the construction industry in the eighties when some businesses went into Germany, thinking construction was the same there as here. They lost their shirt. And they still have that kind of folk memory. So, you need to tap into that, in terms of the need for planning before you go.

In contrast, in the insurance world in the nineties, Irish Life had gone through a lot of change, from being a state company to a private company. They realised as early as 1988 that they needed to own a bank or building society to widen their customer base and enable cross-selling to be delivered. They did eventually acquire Irish Permanent in 1998, but for ten years prior to that the organisation had analysed the scenario over and over. So, balancing analysis and action is important in achieving the right kind of change.

When you go into different industries, you have to consider how to refashion what they are doing to get an effective outcome in a rapidly changing global marketplace. You need to get people to realise that what made them successful in the past may not be what is needed to continue that success into the future. Equally, the organisation must avoid becoming bogged down in over-analysis, which can sometimes cause paralysis. Instead, they need to ensure that within each review and planning process a strong 'bias for action' is present.

What advice do you have for others trying to achieve change?

First, don't make the change be about yourself. It is about getting the people who are in the organisation to understand the change that is needed. After that, you need to become the helper of the bridge building, as opposed to it all being about you having the right answer. There never is just one answer to the problem.

Second, you should try to start with a very small group – four or five – just a sufficient critical mass of people who have a shared view about where they want to take the organisation. I worked with an exceptional leader some years ago and a small group of us, about six in all, successfully drove a radical restructuring and reshaping programme which brought the company back to making profits. He transferred to another company, but didn't pull such a group together there. He ended up quite isolated in his efforts to deliver a similar turnaround and ultimately left. It wasn't that he wasn't a great leader, but, to change complex organisations, I believe that you need a small core of people who can be mutually supportive and mutually challenging, but who have similar ideas about where they want to go. If anybody was really embarking on a change programme, that's what I would say. Get that small core group together, which can be as few as four or five. That seems to be the critical mass required to really drive radical or transformational change, even in large organisations. In doing so, make sure that the breadth of experience and expertise in that group is wide and deep enough to handle any challenges you are likely to encounter.

Third, give yourself sufficient time to plan the change process. The planning stage is the time when you are most in control of the process. I use a checklist. This includes the following:

• Accurate analysis of problem
• Clarity of vision of new entity
• Clear industrial relations negotiation strategy
• Clear communication, contextualisation and information strategy – internal and external
• Clear and realistic timelines
• Secure managerial and board commitment based on understanding of risks
• Clear milestones for delivery
• Focused implementation (identify early visible results)

Put in place a process of objective regular measurement against milestones, coupled with regular internal feedback and communication (particularly of early visible results), to reinforce the commitment and confidence in the change process.

Finally, you should avoid 'sigh of relief' syndrome, which can happen when the main aspects of a change or turnaround programme are achieved and the organisation believes that everything is now sorted. The risk of falling back to former practices can be at its highest when the organisation has gone through huge effort to get the plan implemented, and then takes its eyes off the ball. A key leadership role is to ensure the focus on continuous delivery and improvement becomes an embedded element of the organisation. This delivers and sustains the capacity for true success. Since moving fully into consultancy with my colleagues Teresa and Brian late last year, our practice has been working with our clients in all sectors of the economy to shape and implement significant change agendas, as many organisations focus on achieving true competitiveness in these uncertain times.

5

JOHN LONERGAN

Governor of Portlaoise Prison, 1988–1992; governor of Mountjoy Prison since 1992

John Lonergan is governor of Mountjoy Prison, a closed, medium security prison located in Dublin city centre. Mountjoy is the main prison for Dublin city and the largest prison in Ireland. It houses almost six hundred male prisoners and one hundred women prisoners. In addition to his formal role, John Lonergan is well known for his voluntary work with community and parents' associations.

Career overview and evolution

There is a certain amount of confusion about what a prison governor actually does. The title 'Governor' is a legal term and warrants are made out to the office of the governor of a prison. Governors are then answerable to the courts. In terms of my responsibilities, I am really a manager. I manage Mountjoy Prison, where we have over six hundred men, one hundred women and six hundred staff across different disciplines and professions. Overall, my responsibility is two-fold. One component of it is to ensure that court orders are carried out. What that means is ensuring that the people who are committed to Mountjoy are actually committed and serve the period of time that the law states they should. The second component of my responsibility is that I am answerable to the Minister for Justice or to the director general of the prison service for the day-to-day running of the prison, for the budget and for the management of staff and security.

I joined the prison service by pure accident over forty years ago, in March 1968. At that point, I was green, innocent and young. I had a very simple perspective on the whole thing. I thought that the 'baddies' were in prison and the 'goodies' were outside. I was less than a week in the job in Limerick Prison when I realised that that concept was completely wrong. What I saw there were a lot of unfortunates, a lot of social rejects, a lot of people with serious personal difficulties, psychiatric difficulties, all sorts of difficulties really, and a certain amount of criminality as well, in terms of their behaviour. Overall, it reminded me more of a county home than the vision or expectation that I had of a prison. Since then, I have learnt a huge amount as a result of my life in prison. I've learnt from prisoners, from their families, from staff and from my own reflections. It's had a huge influence on my life and the direction my life took.

Beyond my official role, I also do a lot of voluntary work with communities and with parents' associations. There's no direct linkage between what I do outside of the prison and my job. However, they're interconnected in that a lot of what I talk about is based on my experience. Most of my life experience has been in prison but I don't do what I do outside my job in an official capacity. I involve myself a lot in the community on the basis that I believe that the real solutions to the difficulties we have in prisons will only be found in the community. I believe that we have to look after young people in the community, get them educated and get them equipped to make the best use of their abilities and talents. If you do that, you are far more likely to keep them out of trouble than if you allow them to decay away and end up in prison. I would argue very strongly that far more resources have to be put into prevention rather than responding to crisis.

What drives you?

I grew up in an area in Tipperary where community was very strong, in no small part due to Canon Hayes and Muintir na Tíre.[1] So, living in a

---

[1] A national voluntary organisation dedicated to community development, founded by Canon Hayes in 1937.

community and giving back to a community has always been a basic responsibility for me. And that's what drives me. I believe I've had a unique experience and the best thing I can do is to share it and make clear that there's hope; there's a different way of doing things and we can improve things. That's it in a nutshell.

My passion is about people – trying to save them and ensuring that they don't have to suffer. The people who come to prison suffer, their families suffer and, above all, the victims of crime suffer. So, if we can reduce that and change that then we're saving people and we're making a difference to the lifestyles and quality of life of individuals and their communities. I enjoy my work immensely, which is a plus. A lot of people don't enjoy the job they're doing to any great extent. I have got tremendous personal benefit from it. It has opened my eyes to a whole lot of issues and I have seen both strands of Irish society: I go a lot to disadvantaged areas and I go a lot to the more affluent areas. My own message is quite the opposite in each area. In the affluent areas, I'm saying, 'Look, there's so much that goes on in this world that you don't have a clue about.' In the more disadvantaged areas, I say, 'Just stick with it. There's hope. Get out there. Every human being has talent and ability and it's all about opportunity. If you get the opportunity or ensure your children have opportunity, then that's what will make the change.' So that's what motivates me. I've no passion for prison, because that's a negative thing. I hope that some day we won't need prison at all because it's so negative and destructive.

What does leadership mean to you?

For me, leadership is about the personality and qualities of the leader, the mission and getting the best out of people. Having a mission requires having your own philosophy, values and principles. You need to stand by those, despite any criticism that you might face. If that means challenging people in authority and being unpopular, well, that's what you have to do. So, leadership requires courage. Leaders also need a clear vision. You need to have some idea of what the picture is, the direction that you're going in and how you are going to get there. If you have no long-term big picture and no vision, then you're only moving from day to day. I see a lot of that in the world today. Leadership is also about facilitating others and getting the best out of people. My own leadership hero is Mickey Harte.[2] In the aftermath of an All-Ireland, he said that the enjoyment he got was from observing the enjoyment of other people. I thought that was fantastic. That's exactly what leadership is about. So, for me, it's about bringing a bit of light, hope or good into the life of a prisoner or his family.

In my own role, the biggest single vision I had was to get rid of violence and brutality and to treat all people as equals. Including prisoners. Now, that's not popular. But I don't care and never did care whether it was popular or not. I stand by and stick to the principle that you must start with treating everyone with the utmost respect, even the person who has murdered or maimed or raped. You still start with the basic principle that they're a fellow human being and are entitled to basic human respect. You demonstrate that by how you talk to them, how you deal with them and how you respond to their behaviour and, indeed, misbehaviour. So, for me, a big part of leadership is not being out at the front all the time, but encouraging values in what you're doing and demonstrating those values yourself when dealing with people. So, that is what I stand for and I hope that people pick that up.

For me, the most important thing in leadership is that you have to be yourself. You can learn about the techniques of leadership and management but you shouldn't change yourself or your values. For example, if the system asked me to tell a lie, I wouldn't do it. I will *not* tell a lie. I will *not* spin a story for the system. If we have six hundred prisoners here I will not go out and say the place isn't overcrowded at all or that it is grand. I will say that it is overcrowded. Do we have a drug problem in Mountjoy? Yes! A chronic one. I believe in being honest. Nobody will force me to do anything else.

What has shaped you as a leader?

Some of it has to do with my nature and a lot of it comes from my own life values. I feel that people are entitled to be treated with respect. So, I'm always on the watch in case people are wronged. More broadly, I think that you can enhance people's lifestyles by making their job more interesting

---

[2] Current manager of the Tyrone Gaelic football team.

and fulfilling. That means that they can be happier people. I do try and work with staff around that. For example, when I was moved to Portlaoise Prison in 1988, I arrived in the aftermath of a strike. The staff there told me that they'd never forgive the scabs.[3] Now, the scabs were their fellow workers so I simply said to them, 'Well, I'm sad for you if you're going to remain the next twenty-five years working in Portlaoise, hating a group of people that are your colleagues. If that's the way your life is going to be, you'd be better off leaving.'

How would you describe your own leadership style?

My leadership style depends on the situation. Consultation can be a great way to lead, but sometimes it's a disaster. In a crisis you can't be going around asking people what you should do next. So, for me, my leadership style is about timing and about being able to judge the appropriate thing to do at a particular time. It's about making decisions, it's about being proved right most of the time and it's about being humble some of the time and saying you were wrong. Saying that you were wrong can be a fantastic form of leadership. And people in general tend not to be good at that. I find it very easy now. I found it impossible to say I was wrong twenty-five years ago. But now, as I get older, I think it's a strength to say, 'Jeez, I was wrong actually. You were right.' And, as a matter of fact, that strengthens you.

I think the way that I communicate is an important part of my style; being able to communicate in a way that people respond to. My greatest experience of talking to people was in a crisis where the prisoners were striking over a dispute about a drama project. It was all about a woman who was removed from the drama because of a disciplinary issue. The reaction of all of the rest of the forty prisoners was to say, 'That's it, down tools. We're on strike.' So, the producer came to me and I went down, rounded them all up into a big room and addressed them. I told them all sorts of stuff: that the drama was for them and not for me; that it was nothing but a headache. They ended up giving me a round of applause. And

---

[3] Derogatory term for someone who continues to work despite an ongoing strike in their company or place of work.

you couldn't predict that. Equally, they could have booed me out of the place. So, you see, things happen and you make a judgement and you use whatever skills, experience and strategies that you have. And, when they work, everyone says you're brilliant.

How would those you work with describe you?

I would hope that the prisoners would think of me as somebody who treats them with respect, is fair, would never wrong them and would always be prepared to listen to their side of the story. I also hope that I am able to link with them in times of crisis and be able to identify with their difficulties, whatever they may be. So, I would hope that, on balance, they would always feel that they are treated in a just and fair way, and that they always have someone to go to, even as a last resort, who would listen. I hope the families would feel the same way: that the system is fair and just; that there is no abuse of people; that people are treated with respect and kindness. And kindness is not about handouts. Kindness is a kind word or a kind gesture, all the things that I do my best to practise. We still have prisoners wronged here. But this would never happen on the basis of my support or my instructions for it.

From a staff perspective it's more complex. Sometimes they see me as the Big Bad Wolf. Whether it has to do with cutbacks, duty performance, sick leave or whatever, sometimes the job calls upon you to do things that are not popular. But management isn't about popularity. Some people try to be popular and the staff say, 'He is a lovely guy' or 'She is a lovely person.' But the status they have as a manager might be very low. I would hope that the staff think I am fair. I believe that you can treat everybody within a team as an individual and look after them as individuals. So, if a person is in a crisis, I would say that that individual should take precedence over everyone else. So, if somebody has a family member seriously ill or whatever – irrespective of what is happening – that person is looked after. I believe that, over a period of time, you establish a reputation for being fair and impartial. And maybe the odd time a bit human as well. So, I would hope that staff would say that I am fair and that when they do come to see me that I will listen to them, and that, if they have right on their side, I will come down on their side.

What challenges have you come across in trying to achieve change?

Change can be a very frustrating experience. I learnt a lot about that in the context of the new women's prison.[4]

We had this fantastic vision and philosophy, as well as a new building. But when we moved I was shocked by the resistance from both the prisoners and staff. That resistance came from insecurity and fear. They were losing the structure they were used to. So, from that I began to learn that one of the things that you really need to plan to achieve change is how you are going to move people – not physically, but psychologically and emotionally. That stuff is huge. It's very easy for the person who has the vision to be enthused about a change. You can see the full picture, but what you can forget is that sometimes you're the only one who sees it. So, you must put a lot of effort into getting that vision across to other people.

How do you persuade others to support your vision and goals?

Goals and targets are pretty easy to set. You can write them down and say how you're going to achieve them. You can train, coach and guide people to achieve goals. Indeed, you can nearly force people to move towards achieving them. But the vision thing is deeper, wider and more complex than setting targets. Persuading others to support a vision is really about communication. You have to get the picture across. You have to explain and demonstrate through training, education and all kinds of different ways what you are trying to achieve. Some people are very quick to pick up a vision. Others will always struggle with being able to picture what you are trying to achieve. So, you have to have patience, endurance and a whole lot of absolute belief in your vision. If people are stuck, you have to find out where they and their minds are at before you can start moving them along. Attitude is a huge thing. For example, people who hate prisoners will never be able to fulfil my vision. So, if you have somebody like

[4] The women's prison in Mountjoy opened in December 1999. It has accommodation for eighty people and is called the Dóchas Centre. Dóchas is the Irish word for hope. Although Dóchas is located within the Mountjoy complex, it is situated on the periphery of the grounds, and has a separate entrance. The accommodation is provided in seven separate houses. The centre has been praised for its regime and the positive relationship between the staff and the women.

that, then the first task is to start working on their mindset. Because while they have this antagonistic attitude, they will not be able to identify with a vision that says prisoners should be treated with the ultimate of human respect. So, you have to be very clear in your own mind what your vision is and then you must try to communicate that by demonstration, by example, by training and by all sorts of different techniques. It is a slow process and a difficult one.

What examples do you have of innovation in practice?

I have been involved in numerous initiatives that worked brilliantly here, despite huge resistance at the start. My first major initiative was very innovative at the time. It was to delegate. I can say absolutely that I started the whole system of delegation within a prison because there was none in place before. To change an electric light bulb required the governor to sign a form to direct the trades officer to do it. You can imagine all the reports that were falling on my desk to be signed: fifty electric light bulbs and five taps to be fixed and so on. So, I broke the prison up into wings. I assigned staff of all grades to each wing. The wings operated independently, with myself as a co-ordinator at the centre, pulling it all together. Giving people real responsibility for staff and for managing the wings received fierce resistance. There were votes of no confidence, threats to strike and all sorts of other difficulties. I eventually brought it through, using some amount of force really. In hindsight, if I was back again I'd certainly put more work into my preparation. Green and all as I was at the time, I did put a fair amount of work into preparation. I sent a circular with written information out to everybody. I had the first-ever staff meeting in Mountjoy in 120 years, which was a disaster by the way. I made a disaster of it. But I did make a huge effort to try and get the communication right.

One of the most successful initiatives ever carried out in Mountjoy, and certainly the one with the greatest potential, was a project called the Connect Project. About seven or eight years ago it was introduced under the social funding of the EU. It was all about preparing prisoners to get back into the workplace and the community. It was initiated here and was outstandingly successful. After about four years, it was to be extended out to

Wheatfield Prison[5] and down to Limerick. But, in the middle of the process, there was some obstruction from a few of the professionals involved. That was given bureaucratic credence and recognition, and shortly afterwards the funding was lost. We were doing it in collaboration with the National Rehabilitation Institute and the National Training and Development Institute of Rehab. They were collaborating their programmes and they were fantastic.

After losing something like that, it can be difficult to hear people talking about Thornton Hall[6] as a state of the art prison, because when you think of something like the Connect Project, you realise that we didn't need a state of the art prison to do it. You could do it in a hovel because it was all about people. It was about encouraging people and building up self-esteem and confidence and meeting individual needs. It was all done on a personal basis and in a holistic way. But you just have to keep focused on your vision and personal priorities when things like that happen. At the end of the day, the ordinary prisoner down in the prison is still the number one priority. We have to stay focused on their day-to-day living, helping them to cope with prison life and trying to help them to get back into society on their release.

What difficulties have you experienced in achieving change?

Sometimes I think that everything we have done here has encountered difficulties. Nothing has come in that hasn't been opposed by someone: by staff, by prisoners, by the media, by politicians or by bureaucrats – and sometimes by all of them together. One of our major difficulties is the resistance at prison service headquarters level to any initiatives that show the prisoner in a positive light. It's politically expedient for prisoners to be seen as the baddies. We lost a fantastic work party[7] about twelve months

---

[5] Clondalkin.
[6] The proposed prison development in Swords, Co. Dublin.
[7] The Community Works Party was initiated in 1978 when one prison officer and a small work party of prisoners refurbished a training centre in Rathfarnham. Since then over two thousand prisoners have participated in the completion of various training centres, scout halls and community centres. From the outset, the three main objectives of the Works Party were: 1. to allow prisoners make a positive contribution to local

ago. They were out tending gardens in nursing homes, doing fabulous work for the elderly, for the community and for the prison service. That initiative was withdrawn. There was no support for it, except for the people who were the recipients of it.

Part of the satisfaction of my role lies in reducing and overcoming the obstacles that are put in our way. Genuine obstacles are no trouble because you can explain them and you can get to the root of them. Obstruction for the sake of obstruction can be very difficult because, in other words, people are not interested in any justification or any explanation. They are just opposed to what you are trying to achieve.

How do you achieve change in a constrained public sector context?

Change is almost impossible in the present climate. First of all, prisons will never be top of the pile in terms of popularity. People see prisoners as baddies and there's an overwhelming general attitude which supports that. It's politically expedient and popular and the media play a big role in it as well. So, it is almost impossible to bring out anything that's innovative or that requires funding at the moment. There are huge restrictions on funding across the public sector. To even keep the place going is a major struggle. But I am a public servant and that's the context we're operating in. So, you must understand that and appreciate it and accept it because otherwise it would drive you crazy. And even with understanding that and accepting that, it will still drive you crazy. So, I think you just have to go back to basics. We still have six hundred male and one hundred female prisoners here. That's seven hundred people, and they need to be looked after on a day-to-day basis and they will continue to be the priority. We could enhance what we're doing. We could immensely improve re-offending levels if we had far greater support for education and other activities. We have a very clear idea of what would work and what would be very useful. But we are a million miles away from actually putting that into operation because of a lack of funding.

---

communities; 2. to allow them to experience the value and therapy of working in a positive environment; 3. to place them in a position of trust.

I have to emphasise, though, that it's not always funding that holds us back. There's also a political dimension as well. So, what is good for young fellas may not prove to be politically popular. For instance, training young guys to do some physical activity like boxing might lead to a media headline such as 'Young sex offenders trained how to beat up their victims'. Boxing could be a fantastic activity for those young lads and a therapeutic way to get aggression out of them. But because it's not politically expedient, or popular, it'll never get off the ground. Not because it's not a good therapy or a good programme, but because it wouldn't go down well externally. You can't dwell on such frustrations because, if you do, you'd end up as a bitter and twisted character. And you can't allow the system to do that to you. The important thing is self-preservation. You must preserve yourself to do your best.

What advice do you have for others who would like to bring about change in their own organisations?

People could legitimately say that I haven't made a whole lot of change myself. But if I was to give advice to others I would go back to basics. You must know what change you want, you must visualise it and you must have a very clear strategy and plan to achieve it. You must sell it to as many people as you can and particularly try to convince people in authority. So, you must be persistent and consistent and not doubt yourself. You yourself must put huge effort into it. Passion is a large part of it. You can convince people if you are really, really passionate about something. If you really believe it will work and that it is worthwhile, you have a better chance of success.

Being objective is also very important. Sometimes your passion can take control and there's a difference between blind and informed passion. The real frustration comes when the person with the responsibility or the authority to give it the go-ahead has no belief or interest in what you are trying to do. That can be very frustrating, certainly in the public service where we have no control over budgets at all. When that happens, there's a lot of skills and strategies that can be used. Most important of all is to keep lines of communication open and to avoid making it personal. Neither of those things are easy. You can't hold grudges or be vindictive or anything like that.

What is your vision for the Future of Mountjoy?

Mountjoy doesn't have any vision at all. I suppose that I'm very disappointed to see that the women's prison will be lost with the move to the new prison site.[8] That was a completely new concept. Our vision was to change the whole physical structure, regime and approach to women in prison. And we achieved that. We made fantastic progress and have a huge resource of staff expertise now built up. That expertise and philosophy is spreading out to other prisons as the staff move around. So, I'm very sad to see that going because I don't think it will ever be replaced.

More broadly, my own vision hasn't changed in a quarter of a century. My vision is that, as every prisoner steps in the gate of a prison, their personal needs and requirements in terms of their future, education, treatment or whatever it may be are responded to. We're a million miles away from that at the moment. Prisoners are generally dumped into prisons. Nothing really happens to develop them or to positively occupy them. The vast majority of our prisoners in Mountjoy today are unoccupied. How can you stand up in front of anybody and say that we're fulfilling our service role to the prisoners and the community if we can't even occupy the people? How we occupy them will be the next step then after that. It should be meaningful and it should be educational and it should be beneficial to them.

We have made a lot of progress in some areas. Medical, psychological and psychiatric services have improved. We haven't improved work training and education to the level we should have because the physical facilities are not there. In the longer term, my emphasis will stay on the people rather than the buildings. I don't agree with the focus on state of the art buildings. I've seen the most fabulous buildings with horrific regimes in them, whether they're prisons or hospitals. And I've seen shacks of places falling

---

[8] The Thornton Hall prison complex, which will be located in Swords, North Co. Dublin, fifteen kilometres from Dublin City Centre, will replace Mountjoy Prison. In May 2007 the Léargas consortium was confirmed as the preferred bidder for the public–private partnership (PPP) project. However, in May 2009 talks with the Léargas consortium broke down, necessitating a return to the tender process.

down and fantastic atmospheres in them. Because it's fundamentally about how people are treated. Small little things will never surface in terms of national headlines but can make all the difference in the world on the ground. A lot of the small activities that happen all the time are very beneficial to the prisoners, for instance, very basic stuff like encouraging and facilitating a prisoner to cope with a long sentence, a first-time young offender to cope with his first sentence or an elderly person to cope with his first sentence. All of those small basic things are of massive importance to the individual down in the prison. How does somebody cope with a ten-year sentence at seventy years of age? So it is a huge issue for us to try to help that person cope with it and try to keep him stable and sane. Unless you start off with the core value of respecting people, which informs every approach, then you are not going to make that fundamental difference.

6

BRIAN MAURER

**Former president and medical director of the
Irish Heart Foundation; retired consultant cardiologist,
St Vincent's University Hospital**

Brian Maurer is a clinical cardiologist. He graduated in Medicine from University College Dublin (UCD) in 1964. His postgraduate training began at St Vincent's Hospital, Dublin and continued at the Royal Postgraduate Medical School in Hammersmith Hospital in London. Awarded a British–American Fellowship in 1972, he carried out research and clinical work at the University of Alabama in Birmingham. He returned to Ireland as a consultant cardiologist in 1974 and engaged in clinical practice, research and teaching in various Dublin hospitals until his retirement from public appointments in 2006. He continues to practice as a consultant in cardiovascular disease, based at the Blackrock Clinic.

Amongst other posts, Brian Maurer was chairman of the Hospital Consultants Association and of the publishing committee of the Irish Medical Association in the 1970s and 1980s, and president of the Medicine and the History of Medicine sections at the Royal Academy of Medicine in Ireland in the 1980s. Later, he was president of the Irish Cardiac Society and the Irish Heart Foundation. In February 2010, he retired from the medical directorship of the Irish Heart Foundation.

He is a fellow of the European Society of Cardiology and of the American College of Cardiology.

Brian Maurer participated in the development and implementation of the first cardiovascular strategy, 'Building Healthier Hearts'. He also chaired a ministerial task force which published a report on sudden cardiac death. The recommendations were accepted by Government. He remains active in advising on developments in cardiovascular disease and is a member of a ministerial advisory group on a new cardiovascular strategy.

Career Overview and Evolution

I am a clinical cardiologist and a physician. I went through the usual undergraduate and postgraduate training at UCD and St Vincent's Hospital. Since graduating in 1964, my career has always involved teaching and research, although my primary focus was and remains the treatment of patients. Having completed my internship and having spent a few months in general practice, I spent two years working with renowned heart surgeon Risteárd Mulcahy on the causes of coronary artery disease. I was funded by a research fellowship from the Medical Research Council of Ireland. I am grateful to them and to Professor Mulcahy for the introduction this afforded me to the important role of clinical research in medicine. It also allowed me to spend a few months acquiring some knowledge of the principles of medical statistics and epidemiology by attending a course at the School of Hygiene and Tropical Medicine in London. I then undertook a further period of training in general medicine at St Vincent's before moving to the Royal Postgraduate Medical School in London where I became senior registrar and tutor. While there, my interest moved from general medicine to the emerging specialist area of cardiology.

I was awarded a British-American Fellowship by the American Heart Association and the British Heart Foundation and I spent a year and a half at the University of Alabama. I spent my time there in research, writing papers and getting to know the other twenty members of the faculty. I returned to Ireland in 1974. Since then, I have been engaged in clinical practice in cardiology, teaching and research.

I have always believed that leadership is a major responsibility of consultants in teaching hospitals. For me, the assumption of this role is essential to the proper development of local and national services, particularly in rapidly developing new specialties. As cardiology was such a speciality at the outset of my career, I worked within and without the medical profession to develop and implement policies directed at improving patient care and services.

I was one of the first clinical consultants appointed under the reformed structures set up by the newly established Comhairle na nOspidéal and I was asked to join Gerry Gearty and Risteárd Mulcahy in developing and providing a structured cardiology service for the south of Dublin. To this end, I was appointed to all seven federated Dublin voluntary hospitals, St Kevin's (now St James's) and St Vincent's. Clinical work was mainly in St Vincent's and St James's, with all investigational and interventional activity centred on the Royal City of Dublin Hospital at Baggot St. All major cardiac surgery for the country was carried out at the Mater Hospital, to which I was also attached to integrate surgical and medical services. Given the exponential growth in all areas of cardiology, I think we have fulfilled that brief reasonably well and I am proud that cardiological services in Dublin are comparable to those in any major city. In the south of the city they are now concentrated in the three major successors to the ten small hospitals which existed in 1974: the relocated Adelaide and Meath Hospitals at Tallaght, the other federated hospitals which moved to the redeveloped St James's site, and St Vincent's. They work in close co-operation and, between them, they provide a complete service for nearly 1.5 million people, locally and through national referral.

The appointment of a substantial number of colleagues to all these institutions was an essential part of this service development. With the cessation of the service at Baggot Street in 1987, I concentrated my clinical practice in St Vincent's, but helping the development of services at the successor hospitals continued to be an important part of my work. When the increasing demand for surgery led to the opening of a new unit at St James's, I felt that the task I had been set in 1974 had been largely completed. The challenge now is to respond to advances in practice, which continue with almost bewildering rapidity. When I look back over the thirty-five years since I became a consultant, I think that this capacity to respond appropriately to and to manage change is one of the defining characteristics of leadership.

What drives you?

Need is what drives me. When I was young – and it is the same for most people – I was impatient. But I learnt one very important thing that still keeps me going. You don't measure change in months; you don't measure it in years; you measure it in decades and generations. Bringing about policy change takes credibility, which takes a long time to develop. It also requires some political skills that you only develop with years, and it takes patience and persistence to keep hammering away at something, knowing it is not going to be realised in the immediate future. Part of the reason for that, and its not a bad reason, is that dynamic leaders and innovators very often get taken up blind alleys. You can often end up spending enormous amounts of time, energy and money on areas that aren't productive. So, the people who provide the money and infrastructure to support change prefer to wait and see what the effect of the change actually is. It takes a long time to learn the lesson that you don't achieve change by expertise and enthusiasm. I think I still have a contribution to make through advising my young, enthusiastic and absolutely marvelous colleagues about the direction that they should be taking and the speed at which they should be taking it. There are certain policy initiatives which are needed immediately because they are instinctively right, but there are other changes which might be better implemented more slowly.

I learnt about the inertia associated with policy creation and implementation during the 1980s. In 1969, the small units around the country that were doing occasional cardiac surgery were amalgamated into the Mater Hospital. All of the surgeons went to work there and the change had immediately beneficial results. The risk of a patient dying during heart surgery tumbled and the number of operations which could be done increased dramatically, as the experience and confidence of the surgeons grew. By the early 1980s, we had one of the finest surgical units in Europe. Our results were and still are comparable to anywhere else. But it became clear that the National Surgical Unit couldn't cope with the increasing demand for coronary artery surgery. There were simply too many patients for a single unit. It took us another decade to reverse the decision to have one national unit. The inertia of the system ensured that we couldn't easily undo what we had created, even though it had become clear that it was inappropriate. Of course, when we did it we overdid it. There are eight surgical units in the country now, including the private units, and that's too many. So policy creation is dynamic, but the structures that result from policy creation have to be flexible and they have to be capable of being altered, without leading to a huge dismantling of what's in place.

How do you achieve balance?

I don't think I do achieve balance. If I have one regret looking back, it would be that I didn't get the balance between my professional life and my personal life right when I was younger. My wife would say I still haven't got it right, but I think I have a better balance now. Achieving balance in the medical profession is extremely difficult. There is a duty to provide clinical care. That is paramount and your first obligation. You then also have responsibility for the organisation of the services in your own hospital, in the area for which you are responsible. Then there is the responsibility that we all have as citizens to advise Government and society about any needed changes. Finally, there is the responsibility of ensuring quality control in our work. Getting the right balance between these things is extremely difficult. I once tried to define the functions of a consultant cardiologist and I came up with eighteen different areas of major commitment, if you are to do your job properly. So achieving balance is difficult. I suspect that it is the same for all professions.

What does leadership mean to you?

I think leadership essentially means identifying what is possible to do and develop, identifying the people who can do it and empowering them to do it. We can't all do everything ourselves. The good leader identifies the role that the individual or group with whom he is working can play and then encourages them to develop that role themselves. A leader isn't someone who charges ahead of the regiment. That kind of leader tends to be caught in the gunfire and cut down. So his effectiveness ends very quickly. A leader is someone who encourages the skills of others, harnesses them and is quite often content not to look for formal recognition.

How would you describe your own leadership style?

When I was younger my leadership style was about leading from the front. Curiously, I remember being irritated by people who talked about teams because I thought the responsibility for the delivery of the service was an individual responsibility. It was only as I got older that I came to see that the individual is just a very small proportion of what contributes to an institution. If you do want to deliver a service, you have to harness and focus the individual talents of many people. That's what a team is about and a team leader needs to be able to do that effectively.

What are the critical or key forces that have shaped you as a leader?

One of the key things that has shaped me as a leader is the same motive that brought me into medicine. In fact, I believe that it is the same motive that drives any successful professional. It is an underlying ethos of service. In the case of medicine, it is a service to others, an attempt to heal or to look after those you can't actually heal. Now, people always look a bit cynical when you talk about that as a motive because professionals are generally very well paid. In reality, in most societies there is an underlying assumption that successful professionals will be paid. It is the mechanism of payment that is usually controversial. For the fulfilled professional, that mechanism isn't particularly important – once they have a reasonable standard of living they are usually not driven by a desire to get rich or be affluent.

Is there anything that could have made you a more effective leader?

When I look back at myself and how I was, I think that I would have been more effective had I been more patient, if I had listened more and if I had been quicker to learn at the beginning. I also think that I would have been more effective if I hadn't diffused my interests so widely. That does take a toll – physically and otherwise. I had an illness when I was forty, which made me change my whole career dynamic. It made me realise the benefit of being focused on the development of your own area. For example, in medicine, if you are trying to develop services in a particular area, it is probably not a good idea to get heavily involved in the representative bodies for the profession. It is not a good idea to become involved in, say, the Royal College of Physicians, the governing body of the Irish Medical Organisation, active politics, local politics or even national politics. These are all options, but by and large you have enough work to do looking after your own patch. I base this on my own personal experience. I did make the mistake of being far too involved in too many things. After I was ill, I had to refocus and drop an awful lot of what I was involved in. Doing that made me a lot more effective.

What, in your opinion, are the characteristics of effective leaders in healthcare?

When I look back over the years I think that persistence and the ability to learn are the traits that have made people effective. In fact, I think that slow learning is often very helpful. Fast learners tend to be very bright and can often intuitively grasp the solutions to the problems. But, equally, they may chase up blind alleys. Those who learn slowly tend to benefit from the experience which comes with maturity. Their confidence and ability to lead tends to come from lessons which they have learnt in the past rather than from the intuitive appreciation of what may be done and the frustrations which come from that. So, you will often find that people who are most effective are those who have taken the long route to leadership. They are often in the background as youngsters and not the auditors of the Literary and Historical Society,[1] for example. You often find that the people who sat in the back row listening are running the country thirty years later. Some of the auditors do too, of course.

In a broader sense, being an effective leader in healthcare requires that doctors and others aren't focused on their own individual speciality, that they take a broader view of healthcare delivery. For example, take a hospital with twenty specialities. If each speciality has three or four consultants who are extremely zealous, highly intelligent and effective, you can imagine the types of struggles that would ensue if each was competing for scarce resources. You can also imagine how tunnel vision can develop – if you get to the stage when only your own area matters. So, it is impor-

---

[1] The college debating society of UCD.

tant that doctors should engage with management, but that the engagement takes a broader view. And it is equally important that institutions should be able to take or adopt policies which allow them to integrate into the national or regional picture.

It distresses me when I see conflicts that have arisen between hospitals. They are perfectly understandable, but it is actually very damaging. At the end of the day, we have to refocus on why we are here, what we do and how best we can set out to help the people we are trained to help. I think one of the most important things we must do in becoming effective in this way is to develop the ability to listen to what the other side is saying.

What do you look for in the people you work with?

I look for truth, honesty, capacity for self-analysis and self-criticism, a willingness to learn and a willingness to raise questions. All organisations need people who will question. That is particularly the case in hospitals where the senior people need to be questioned and challenged, in a pleasant fashion, by the youth. There is a lot of truth in the wonderful fable *The Emperor's New Clothes.*[2] We can get to a stage where we just assume that what we are doing is right. When we are at that stage, it is very rare that we will be challenged.

The Neary case[3] is one such case very much in the public record. I think the great tragedy of that case was that nobody challenged Michael Neary. I don't think that something like that could have happened in a unit where there were five or six people providing the service that Dr Neary was supposed to provide on his own. It wouldn't have happened in any unit where there was real consultation between the doctors and the nurses, some of whom, in the case of Neary, appeared to have seen what was going on. So,

---

[2] Hans Christian Andersen tale about two weavers who propose to make a suit for the Emperor from material that only the most worthy can see. Out of pride, the Emperor pretends he can see the suit and so do his ministers. In the end, when he parades out in front of his people in his 'suit', he is actually naked.
[3] Michael Neary is a retired consultant obstetrician/gynecologist, who preformed an inordinate amount of caesarian hysterectomies, without consent, during his time at Our Lady of Lourdes Hospital in Drogheda, Co. Louth. His actions led to an inquiry by the Minister for Health and Children.

I think the medical profession learnt a great deal from that, as it should. I don't think it can happen again. But my key point is that we need to put in place structures where review, questioning and challenging is part of day-to-day work processes. The leaders need to accept that they should be challenged and will be challenged and that it is a good thing that they are challenged. And the seniors, trainees and the people in the middle who do most of the work need to be empowered to discuss or challenge when necessary.

How would people you work with describe you?

I have retired from my public appointments. I was very touched when I retired by the affection people seemed to have for me. I was touched by the fact that, when I do go back to hospitals I have worked in, I am greeted very warmly and made feel very welcome, and by the fact that I am asked in to teach from time to time. But I know this wasn't always the case. I know a lot of people found me very difficult to work with. I believe I had a reputation among some young trainees as being so exacting that some people simply didn't want to come and work with me. Maybe that wasn't a bad thing.

Do you think that there is a difference between leadership and management?

I think there is a huge difference between leadership and management. Management is the process of applying skills to the discharge of certain functions, whereas leadership encompasses that but also entails bringing people with you. It also means you have to sit around a table with ten to twenty people with different interests and be able to bring them in a particular direction, provided it is the right thing for them to do. That means you have to be able to relate to and understand each person and what they do. You also have to be able to debate with them and be mature enough to know that, when a consensus just doesn't emerge, it is unlikely that your vision is right and you will have to go back and revise it. A lot of people have executive gifts that allow them to run specific functions, but not all managers can be leaders because not all people have the same kind of gifts.

However, all can participate in the process of leadership. Now, that may seem to be contradictory, but the development and evolution of a leader within a team is actually the creation of all the members of the team. I have been fascinated watching some of my successors. I have seen their leadership skills emerging and seen how they have gradually grown in the esteem of those who work with them and around them. That's one of the reasons I have come to believe that growth, both personal and institutional, may often be better if it's not too fast.

What advice do you have for aspiring leaders?

If I were to offer advice based on my own career, I would emphasise the realisation that other people had as much if not more to offer than I had in terms of being able to develop, think and deliver ideas. Therefore, you have to get away from the idea that you are the great individual that knows everything and tap into the collective abilities of the people with whom you are working. I think that applies in every field and I wonder if that is perhaps the defining feature of leadership.

How have you achieved policy change?

The national cardiovascular strategy

The Irish Cardiac Society was founded in 1949 and has always represented the cardiac specialists in the country. When I first joined, it was a very small group of people, as we had only about fifteen to seventeen physicians who had a major interest in cardiology. As things developed over the years, it became a forum in which we discussed many issues facing the profession and the speciality as a whole.

Then, by the early 1990s, it became apparent that the country was not sufficiently keeping pace with the major developments in the speciality. There were a number of reasons for that. One of them was that there was a need for clearly defined leadership to inform Government and civil society as to what was available, what could be done and how it ought to be done.

So, by 1992, a group of us decided we would sit down and present a plan for the development of good cardiac services in the country to the Irish Cardiac Society. We had formulated that by 1994 and then began to encounter enormous difficulty in getting this on the table for discussion. We wrote to the then Minister for Health several times, but it took us two and a half years to get a response. Ministers are very busy people. But when we did get a response, it was a major one. The Minster set up a group, which produced the cardiovascular strategy a couple of years later, essentially with the blueprint which we had written. So, for many of us that was a demonstration of what you can do if you set about informing people of needs, justifying the needs, doing the economic analysis and then essentially lobbying, thereby gaining recognition and eventually achieving implementation.

That approach is now being replicated in the area of stroke care. This was an offshoot of the cardiovascular strategy as stroke is a cardiovascular disease. However, at the time when the cardiovascular strategy, with its two hundred and twelve points, was adopted by Government, stroke was put to one side as it was felt it needed further examination. At the time, it was stated that the Government would later produce a stroke strategy, but they didn't. And so, by default, we had to do it again. Only this time it wasn't just the cardiologists again, it was a much broader constituency. It was the stroke people, the rehabilitation people, the geriatricians, the nurses, the speech therapists – everybody. The Irish Heart Foundation Council, which represented all these groups, did an audit of the stroke services within the country and on the basis of that audit we produced the blueprint for the stroke strategy, which is now going to the Minister for Health for consideration.

What difficulties have you encountered in achieving change?

As I emphasised, I have learnt that change occurs over decades and generations. Ninety per cent of what I have tried to do hasn't been accomplished at the speed I wanted. So, what you have to do in the end is settle for what can be accomplished and bring people along with you. Even when you go outside your own field, you have to be able to present your case in a reasonable manner, a truthful manner. When you are dealing with people who are entrusted with the actual management of the state and management of policy, you have to realise that their responsibilities are totally different to your own. You have responsibilities to your patients, your institution and with regard to policy, but at the end of the day you are not the person who is elected by the citizens to effect all these things. So, you have to learn how to be patient while you bring about consensus on what should be done and you must learn how to be disappointed.

How do you encourage people to support your vision?

For me, this is about education and persuasion, which are helped by having integrity and aspiring towards truthfulness, trustworthiness and honesty. Of course, none of us ever lives up to these aspirations totally. However, you can tell if people have integrity. You know them by instinct and can especially tell if you are sitting around trying to work with them over a long period of time. Reputations for that sort of thing are not lightly won. That's why you have to be very patient. I remember an anecdote that was told to me by a now retired financial controller in one of the hospitals where I worked. The year after I was appointed I went to the secretary manager of the hospital and delivered a rant on what I needed and why it was needed in order to develop the department. It was a relatively small sum of money. And the retired financial controller told me that, after I left, they both had a good laugh and said that I would learn not to be so enthusiastic.

How do you bring about policy change?

You must have a goal towards which you are working. Policy change must be directed towards achieving the aims of the institution or service. Policy should only be changed when things become inappropriate or detract from the purpose of the institution. Now, that's not as rare as you think. For instance, hospitals in my view have become inappropriate vehicles for the development and delivery of many services to patients. It has become quite clear over the last decade that many services are best delivered on an outpatient basis or maybe at a physically different location. But our institutions haven't got to the stage where they see that yet and the process of changing from an inpatient, ward delivered service to an outpatient service is a slow but good process of change.

Once you have a clear view of what you are working towards, you need to develop a consensus on the need for change. When the consensus has been reached among the people who are most directly involved, you try to persuade those who are not directly involved. When you have persuaded them, you then move to persuade whoever is responsible for implementing the change. If there is a need to develop funding, you need to consider whether there are competing interests with other groups involved in the same institution. If there are, you need to try and develop a consensus with them. That entails ranking everyone's aims in order of priority. Because if you go to funding authorities with competing claims from within the same institution, and they are not agreed on by the institution, you get absolutely nowhere. That is a classic reason for failing to get something done. So, you must first of all get agreement within your own area as to what is needed, then you must get agreement within the institution on the needs of the institution and the order in which those needs are ranked. Then you must go and persuade those who are responsible for giving you the funding or capacity to undertake the initiative. If you take the cardio-vascular strategy as an example of a policy initiative that worked, it was because every cardiologist in the country signed up to it irrespective of where they worked. Nobody dissented. And so, when we went to Government to make our case, they couldn't ignore us. It was clearly a well-developed, thought-out and reasoned policy. That's why it worked.

What advice do you have for others who wish to bring about change?

Be patient. In 1974 was informed that I would have my new investigative cardiac laboratory by 1977. We eventually opened it in 1987. So, recognise that things take time but do eventually happen. You should also think care-fully about what you want to do and how you want to do it. Don't ever change just for the sake of changing. Consider the fact that what you are trying to change has been developed and has evolved over quite a long period and therefore be quite sure that what you are trying to put in its place will actually achieve what you want. When you have decided that this is the case, test your ideas by consulting your peers or those who know a lot about the idea. Then, test your case on those who don't know so much about the idea. They are the people who will ensure that your case fulfils common sense criteria. Then you have to go out and begin the process of trying to bring about change.

7

Sr Stanislaus Kennedy

Founder and life president of Focus Ireland; founder of The Sanctuary; founder of the Immigrant Council of Ireland and Young Social Innovators

Sr Stanislaus Kennedy, or Sr Stan as she is more affectionately known, is one of Ireland's best-known social innovators. She has been a member of the Congregation of the Religious Sisters of Charity since 1958. Since then, she has initiated, developed and championed a range of social innovations focused on addressing exclusion, in all its forms. During the 1960s she helped to establish Kilkenny Social Services. In the 1970s she became a founder member of the National Federation of Youth Clubs and of the School of Education in Kilkenny. In the 1980s, she founded Focus Ireland, a charity for homeless people. In the 1990s, Sr Stan founded The Sanctuary, a meditation and spirituality centre in the heart of Dublin City. In 2001, she founded the Immigrant Council of Ireland and Young Social Innovators. She is on the board of the Community Foundation for Ireland. She is also a prolific writer and her books include: Now Is the Time *(TownHouse, 1998),* A Bundle of Blessings *(St Pauls, 1999),* Gardening the Soul *(TownHouse, 2003),* Seasons of the Day *(TownHouse, 2003), and* Stillness through My Prayers *(TownHouse, 2006). Sr Stan has received many awards and accolades for her work on behalf of the marginalised, including Kerry Person of the Year,*

the Lord Mayor of Dublin's Award and the Meteor Humanitarian of the Year Award. She has received honorary doctorates in Law from Trinity College Dublin, University College Dublin and the Open University.

Career Overview

My work takes me into different areas of need and I work with four different organisations which I've been involved in setting up. Focus Ireland provides services, research and advocacy for people out-of-home. It is now one of the biggest voluntary bodies working with homeless people in Ireland. I was the chief executive for nearly ten years. I then decided that it was time to move on. I took a non-executive role with the organisation and was appointed as life president by the board. I've maintained my role on the board of directors and continue to work alongside and support the organisation.

The Immigrant Council of Ireland works with and for migrants. It conducts policy and research work and provides information, support, advocacy and strategic litigation to migrants. I set up this organisation in 2001. I work alongside the organisation in a supportive capacity. I sit on the board and I also help with fundraising, training and other matters.

I also set up the Young Social Innovators in 2001. That provides a social awareness and active citizenship[1] programme for young people between fifteen and eighteen years of age. I have been involved in running it from the beginning and am quite involved in the organisation and its activities.

Finally, The Sanctuary is a spirituality centre in the heart of the city. The idea is that it's a place in the city where people can go to get rest and where they can find silence and stillness.

For me, the balance between my work and my life has always been a challenge. On the one hand, I am very much drawn into activities and organisations, while there is also a part of me that is very much attracted by silence and stillness. That part of me has been there from the beginning. I've always, even when I was very young, had a need for time apart and by myself. Over the years, I have tried to work out a way in which I could have that time. The Sanctuary is an example of how I saw a broader need for

---

[1] A concept that embodies formal and non-formal, political, cultural, inter-personal and caring activities.

balance. About ten years ago I started thinking about people, particularly those involved in the caring area, who have a lot of demands on their time – physical and emotional demands. I felt that there was a need for a place they could go to be refreshed, to be restored and to have silence and still-ness in their lives. And that's how The Sanctuary developed. It continues to provide that for people in the caring area. It is also reaching many others. For example, there's a big demand from school children who come to learn how to meditate. The Sanctuary expresses what I needed myself and what I thought was needed by others. We say that we bring stillness to the world. I sit on their board and I teach short six-week courses on meditation a few times a year.

I try to have balance in my involvement with the different organisations and be clear to myself about the way that I'm going to be involved. For example, two years ago I decided that I would become involved in the coffee shop down on Eustace Street. This was the first part of Focus Ireland that was established in 1985. I work there one morning a week. It's a nice way to continue my direct involvement with out-of-home people.

Overall, my work is quite varied and has changed a lot over the years. I started out being directly involved in running organisations. Now, I work more alongside them, participating and helping in different ways.

What has motivated and directed you during the evolution of your career?

My motivation really comes from my faith and my belief that we're all equal, we're all made in the image of God, we're all brothers and sisters, and together we form the body of Christ. That's a very strong motivation. It really helps me to put my best forward and enables other people to give their best too. I joined the Sisters of Charity because I wanted to work with the poor. My understanding of poverty is very much about exclusion. People are poor when they haven't got what is normal in society. So, if it's normal for people in society to have two coats and to have two pairs of shoes and to be able to participate in their community and to feel respected, wanted and that they belong, then people who haven't got that are poor. Whether they are children or whether they are adults, whether they are Irish or whether they are migrants, whether they are young or old doesn't matter. What matters to me is the fact that they are excluded and margin-alised. I see and continue to see myself as somebody who can do something to lessen that exclusion.

I have remained in the Sisters of Charity because it appeals to me spir-itually. The spiritual way of life has become the resource that enabled me to reach out to others, so I was actually lured by God into work that appealed to me. I suppose that the activity was present in my life from the beginning, but I saw that I had a great need to develop spiritually if I was going to continue in that work.

What does leadership mean to you?

I think that a leader knows where he or she is going while a manager knows how to get there. Leadership and management are different. Lead-ership is about empowering while management is more focused on control. Stephen Covey, the author of *The Seven Habits of Highly Effective People* (Simon & Schuster, 1989), captures this distinction well. He tells a story about people cutting down trees in the jungle. The leader gets up to the top of a tree and shouts down, 'We're in the wrong jungle' and the man-ager shouts back, 'Leave us alone. We're getting a lot of work done.' So, I do think that leadership is about empowering. I think that's true whether for individual leaders or for leadership in general. It also is a very central concept when it comes to working with the poor because, of all things, the poor are disempowered and powerless in relation to systems and structures.

My own leadership style is centred on empowering. Empowering requires being able to see the bigger picture and to envision a different future, a different kind of reality – for people and society. I think that some people have a vision for themselves and some people haven't. Some people go through life and don't even know what their vision for themselves is. That's just the way they are. Neither do they have a vision for their com-munity or society. But I think that it is very important to have a vision and to work towards it. In fact, I think you can't have leadership without a vision. The vision of Focus Ireland, for example, is that everybody has a right to a place called home. And how I got that vision at the beginning was that, during 1983–4, I did some research on the nature and extent of homelessness amongst women in Dublin. I then spent a year with eight young women who were homeless. That was a year when I wanted to really understand what it was like to be homeless. I felt that I didn't understand the homeless and that, if I was going to achieve anything, I was going to have to understand them better.

The year I spent learning from those eight women was the greatest year of my life because I really did grow to understand what it was like to be out of home. I spent the first half of the year listening to those women describe the awfulness of being without a home, of not having a place to put your things, not having a door to lock after you or a place where you could wash and dress. But the most important thing that they described was the awfulness of not being respected, of losing their sense of themselves, their self-esteem, their self-respect and their self-pride. They lost that quickly once they became homeless because of the way people treated them. And they could count on one hand, or maybe one finger, the people who had showed them respect. Respect was critically important to them and they taught me that. They taught me that, no matter what we did going forward, we had to develop a service that would restore people's pride, restore their respect and restore their self-esteem.

As the year went on, I asked them more directly about what was needed in Dublin for homeless people. They said very clearly that there was no 24-hour phone service to contact and get information, there was no place for people to drop into to get information and advice, and there was no place where women could go and eat. There were mostly men in the dinner centres and there was a lot of aggression and violence. So, they were afraid to go there. These women needed a place to go to get good food and sit down and feel safe from street values. And they said that there were no people on the streets who they felt they could trust. They needed people who would reach out to them on the street. Those were exactly the services we established when we started Focus. We tried to have an organisation that would be inclusive and would include them. We called it Focus Point because it was a point of focus in their lives. That name was kept for about ten years until the service went nationwide. We then changed the name to Focus Ireland.

Those women and that experience taught me that, if there was going to be an organisation and if I was going to lead it, I had to clearly identify why we were doing it and what our vision was. Now, when I'm doing any training with Focus, I always say that I was taught by those homeless people that you really have to listen to and be led by the people in need. They're the only ones that know what it's like to be on the receiving end and they're the people who will teach us. I think leadership has to emerge that way. I also think that another way of leading is to provide opportunities for people to find themselves and to find their own gifts. That's very important because out of that emerge new leaders.

What has shaped you as a leader?

When I was young I was sent to Kilkenny to work with Bishop Peter Birch. He was a very liberal man, committed to the poor and very committed to developing participatory communities where people could show their care. In Kilkenny we developed structures so that people and volunteers could become involved in the community and care for their own people in need.

I also learnt that people need a lot of support in their work and that we shouldn't expect them to be overly extended in their commitments or to do things that are beyond them. So, in order to develop organisations, you have to ensure that people have the right kinds of skills and to help people find the right kind of training and education. And I think I learnt that from Bishop Birch. He was very particular about the kinds of support that were given to volunteers and others who came to work. From a very early age I became involved in training. I helped to set up the School of Social Education in Kilkenny, which became a training centre for childcare workers. Later, through my work in Focus Ireland, in the Immigrant Council and in Young Social Innovators, one of the things I would be very particular about was ensuring that there was the right kind of opportunities for the staff to be trained and that they had the right kind of supervision and support to enable them to give their best. Having a good system of support and supervision makes a good organisation.

In Kilkenny I learnt about providing the kinds of structures that enable people to care and the kind of support that enables staff to flourish. That model and my experience in helping to set up services in Kilkenny were big influences in terms of the direction my life took.

How would those who work with you describe you?

I think people would see me as somebody who is highly motivated, with a clear vision and mission and a capacity to see the bigger picture. I think I would also be seen as somebody who is not just a social service person, but who also wants to change the systems that cause injustice in the first place. I suppose people would see me as somebody who understands that we're just one organisation that's doing something but that there's a bigger picture out there, and deeper causes to the problems that we're trying to respond to. Therefore, as well as responding to the need, we should be tackling the causes and we should be putting pressure on those who have the power and authority to change those causes. So, if we're doing something about homelessness, clearly the problem has to do with a lack of housing and that means that we must also always challenge the system. When I was the first chairperson of the Combat Poverty Agency, we were very committed to doing something about the structures that cause poverty. I suppose people would also see me as somebody who cares and who would have certain compassion, especially towards people who have very little.

What, in your opinion, are the characteristics of effective leaders in the voluntary sector?

I think leaders in the voluntary sector have to have a good understanding of the society in which we live and of the systems that we have. We also need to be able to see the wider picture beyond our own organisation and have the capacity to think outside the box. In particular, we have to be able to let go when we have done certain work. It is better if we can pass it on. For example, if the state can do it then we can move on to the next thing. I think that is also the case on an individual level. For me, it was very important that I moved on from being in charge of an organisation to being able to support it in another way. That gave opportunities for other people to take on leadership roles in Focus and elsewhere. If I had remained in charge, they might never have been able to develop their leadership skills. It is important to know when to let go and move on.

At an organisational level, leadership in the voluntary sector has to be co-operative. Voluntary organisations can't afford to be in competition with one another and have to see the complementarities of each other's work. That makes giving and gaining the co-operation of others very important.

Achieving innovation and improvement in organisations: how do you overcome difficulties?

I have encountered many difficulties in my work, but the ones that really come to mind are the ones that have to do with poverty. Poverty is a very big issue and its resolution requires societal and structural change, which are very difficult to bring about. For example, in the early stages in Focus we tried very hard to listen to people who were homeless and to develop our services out of that. And one of the things that emerged was the need for emergency accommodation for young people. We had young people coming to the coffee shop and the day centre, but there wasn't a place for them at night. Putting accommodation in place was a big project and would have cost a quarter of a million a year to run. That was in 1990, so it was a lot of money. For three years we tried everything we could think of to get the Health Board to agree to undertake this. Finally, I got the Sisters of Charity to fund the service for one year. And they also gave a premises. Once they had agreed to provide that, I went back to the Minister and asked him if he would come in behind it if we did it for a year. He did come in behind it, but it was an uphill struggle. Of course, the centre has been full since the day it opened and many more centres have opened since.

I think myself, and I have always thought, that people only see problems when they should try to see solutions. When I was in college, I was told that you should define the problem and then develop the response. But I think that it is actually only when people see that there is a solution – a way out – that they can see the problem. And I can say that about all of the services I have been involved in from the very beginning. For example, when I was setting up Focus I wanted to get supportive housing for people who were out of home because they weren't capable of running their own home due to all kinds of mental health needs. I went around talking to different government departments about the need for supportive housing. And they asked whether I meant a hostel or housing. I kept saying that I meant something in between but they couldn't get it. It was only when I was finally given a convent by the Sisters of Charity that the Minister for the Environment gave money in the budget, a million pounds, to convert it. Once it was complete, people said, 'Of course that is what was needed.' Now supportive housing for homeless people is all over the country. But, at that stage, because people couldn't get their heads around the way of resolving it, they couldn't see the problem. So, I do believe that a leader really must take those kinds of risks and develop a solution, even if there isn't backing for it. Solutions allow people to see a need.

How do you gain support and resources for change initiatives?

I think developing solutions and showing a way forward is most definitely the best way to gain support and resources. It is about announcing as well as denouncing; I think, if you announce as you denounce, you are more effective. The second thing that is important is to try to get the attention of key people who will really come behind certain issues. There are people who will support some issues, while others will support different issues. Being able to identify who could be the champion for a particular initiative is important. That entails thinking about who you can go and talk to, and who will be willing and able to say what you are saying in a different way and a way that appeals to other audiences. That works well, but takes a lot of thinking through and a lot of work. I think it's also important to realise that people really like to see success and they like to see that what they are supporting works. So, I think that it's important to use opportunities to help people to see that what they're supporting is valuable. I think we owe that to people who support us, whether they support us financially or in other ways. We owe it to them to let them know what it is that they are supporting and what they have brought about.

What advice do you have for others who would like to bring about change?

I think the first thing you have to do as a leader is to listen. Anybody who wants to be in leadership should listen to the people who are on the margins because they understand society much better than those of us who are in the middle of it. I think that being able to listen and to take on board what people are saying are the most important leadership qualities.

8

MARK ROWE

General practitioner and managing partner in the Rowe Creavin Medical Practice, Waterford Health Park, Waterford City

Mark Rowe is a graduate of University College Dublin (UCD) medical school. He did his specialist training in general practice and became a qualified member of the Irish College of General Practitioners in 1995, achieving the first place Ellard Eppel Award. Since then he has worked as a GP in Waterford City.

He has given seminars and has acted as a guest speaker on the topic of men's health at a number of events. In 2008, he wrote The Men's Health Book – A Guide for the Irish Man *(Blackhall Publishing), all royalties from which go to the men's cancer division of the Marie Keating Foundation.*

The Waterford Health Park (www.whp.ie) which he owns and developed, opened in 2009. This is a restored AWN Pugin-designed[1] former convent, which has been transformed into a 30,000 square foot primary healthcare facility. This building has been included in the Irish Government's policy document, Architecture – Quality in the Built Environment 2009–2014.

Mark Rowe is the Irish representative in the Caritas Project, which is an international collaboration of healthcare centres based on the principle of generative

---

[1] Augustus Welby Northmore Pugin (1812–1852) was an English architect and designer.

space. This is a new leading-edge paradigm in healthcare design, which looks at the sustainable benefits of providing inspiring surroundings in the healthcare set-ting and the resultant long-term health improvements for individuals. Mark Rowe is also on the judging panel of a new global annual award programme, called 'A Place to Flourish: The Generative Space Health Improvement Award'.

In 2007, he ran the New York Marathon and fundraised for two charities. He is the team doctor for the Waterford Senior GAA Hurling team.

Career Overview

I work on a number of levels. First of all, I am a GP – basically, a family doctor. The difference between GPs and hospital doctors is that we spe-cialise in people and try to provide cradle-to-grave care in our communities, over time. It's a great privilege to serve my local community and that's something that continues to inspire me in my work. I believe strongly in trying to merge health with education at every opportunity, by providing interactive health talks. As well as that, I'm the leader of a multidisciplinary practice. We started, back in 1999, with just four people. And that has grown over the last ten years or so into a practice with twenty-five staff. So, there is obviously a management role there. Another area is our role in young GP and medical student education and training, which is a great way to stay energised in practice as their enthusiasm is contagious.

The thing I like most about my work is being able to make a difference. I think, for me personally, as a GP, there is huge job satisfaction which you can't measure. You can go in and audit a GP practice and look at the com-puter records, and look at statistics, but they can't measure the process, the intangible quality of the interaction between a doctor and a patient. So there's huge job satisfaction in helping people. I also love the autonomy that we have in general practice and I can empathise with some of my hos-pital colleagues who can't seem to be able to break out of the quagmire of loss of control and lack of autonomy. They can't really develop their own services because they are sometimes stymied – whether by medical politics, by funding issues, by management or by competing services. In contrast, as GPs, we have a large degree of control over our practice, which is great. And I'd be very, very slow to ever give that up. Of course, the flip side of this is that, as a small business, you have to be customer-focused and adaptable.

What has motivated and directed you in the evolution of your career?

My career has been influenced by those around me, by my own drive and motivation, and by one transformative experience early in my career. My grandfather was a doctor and I can remember saying as a little boy that I was going to be a doctor when I grew up. Now, I don't know whether that was because he was a role model for me or whether I was conditioned, or if it was just in my genes. But I never really wanted to do anything else. I always loved the idea of helping people and still am very interested in people and their stories. I love understanding what makes people tick and being able to help them − whether it's medical help or a bit of advice or counselling. I gain so much from that. Although I am a doctor, I was also very influenced by my late father, who was head of the business school in Waterford Institute of Technology. He always spoke about the great people he had around him and had great respect for his secretary and colleagues. I learnt a lot about people management from him and particularly about the value of working in a team.

I've always been a very driven person and that has influenced my career. I remember back in school if I got 98 per cent in a test, I'd want to know where the 2 per cent went. And I think that's a double-edged sword. It can be a great strength to be driven, but the flip side is that you need to know and be able to measure when you've achieved something tangible. Otherwise, you can be always chasing the next thing without being sure of whether you've succeeded at anything.

We started our own practice ten years ago and things were going fine. We were growing and I think that a bit of complacency could have set in. But we had a transforming experience when we were in practice a year. One night, two guys broke into our practice. It was a small premises over a shop. They broke in and burned the place out. So, we were victims of an arson attack. We got a call from the gardaí at 7.30 a.m. the following morning and arrived to see the whole place up in smoke. That has had a lasting effect on me. We had put everything into setting up that new practice. Even some furniture from our first house was in there because it was all-hands-on-deck to start the new business. I suppose what I learnt from that is that nobody owes you a living. You can't get complacent and you can't rest on your laurels. I decided that day that we were going to build our own place.

I learnt that, ultimately, the only person you can change in this life is yourself. You can't expect others to change and you can't expect others to do it for you. You have to do it for yourself.

How do you achieve balance in your own life?

Although I am driven, I think I have good balance. Being involved in primary healthcare can give you a great sense of perspective. It can be very humbling to see the challenges that some people deal with day in and day out – overcoming adversity in many situations in life. So that helps to keep me grounded. I also love exercise. I believe that exercise is the greatest pill of all. As a doctor you should lead by example. I love playing tennis, going for a walk with my wife Edel and I love spending time with my kids. I'm also the team doctor for the Waterford GAA Senior Hurling team. I never cease to be amazed by the passion, energy and drive that these guys bring to their sporting performance. It's a great privilege to be in a dressing-room with them. So, I think that all of that helps to give me a sense of balance and a sense of perspective.

What does leadership mean to you?

For me personally, leadership involves having big dreams and not being afraid of having them. I think that's really important. And I also think that leadership involves being prepared to take risks. They may be large or small risks, but most important of all is that you believe in them. So, for me, leadership is moving with what you believe in. As a leader, I also think that you have to set an example and follow through on your commitments to your colleagues and your staff. In doing that, it's the small things that can make a big difference.

I like the saying that the direction of the ship is more important than the speed of the journey. I like to be quite consultative in how we go about getting things done. It's best to involve others in the decision-making process. In our practice, we have regular meetings and an AGM every year, which is a meeting for three hours on-site. All the members of our team attend, so that's about twenty-five staff. We closed the practice for our last one and had a doctor on call with an emergency number, in case that was required. We all sat down and did a SWOT analysis[2] on our move to our new practice site at the Waterford Health Park. We looked at what was going well in that process, what needed to change, and identified our strengths, weaknesses, opportunities and the issues facing us. Everybody has an equal say in those meetings and all contributions are valued. I read Nelson Mandela's book *The Long Walk to Freedom* several years ago. And he described a leader as being like a shepherd, who leads from behind. I liked that because you have to have your team on board with you. Without your team, you are nothing. Of course you do need to know where you're going. So, that is why I have tried to adopt a consultative style in my own work and also tried to introduce formal processes and mechanisms for consultation in the practice.

When I think of the healthcare system, I think leadership requires having a clear mandate for primary care. Barbara Starfield, the American health economist, has shown that, for every dollar you invest in primary care, you can save ten dollars in the overall health system. So, you might think, 'That's a no-brainer. Why don't we do that in the morning?' The reason is that politics and funding has traditionally favoured the hospitals. And funding has often followed inefficiencies in healthcare. In a way, the more inefficient services in hospitals are able to attract more resources. And primary care has traditionally got crumbs. And it's not about making doctors richer. It's about putting the infrastructure into primary care. That would allow chronic disease such as diabetes, asthma and heart disease to be treated much more cost-effectively through general practice. It would also allow patients to be treated closer to home. So, it would add value for patients too. A true win-win scenario!

What has shaped you as a leader?

As I mentioned earlier, I was very influenced by my father and my own experiences here, particularly the arson attack on our first practice prem-

---

[2] Analysis under the headings strengths, weaknesses, opportunities, threats.

ises. That has helped me to learn how to deal with disappointment. I'm idealistic and driven and the other side of those is that you can feel let down or disappointed when things don't work out as you have planned them. I've learnt more from the mistakes I've made and the things that I should have done differently than from the things that went well. I also think that going to boarding school at the age of twelve really taught me to stand on my own two feet and gave me a lot of independence.

What, in your opinion, are the characteristics of effective leaders?

I think effective leadership is all about communication, working with people towards a common objective and having shared goals and values. So, when I think of leaders in healthcare, I think of people who are great advocates for their patients, people who are very clear in their purpose, who stick with the message, who focus on the long-term objectives. And people who can use the media in a positive way to get clear health messages across. There have been great champions in healthcare down through the years who have had a mission and delivered on that. People like Bill Shannon, the late James McCormack and Michael Boland spring to mind as outstanding Irish doctors in that regard. But I think that we need a lot more leadership in healthcare. That should come from the doctors. We need to engage much more on a cross-sectional basis, with education, with research and with our communities, so that we can all work together to build something better for us all. I also think that healthcare needs to be demystified. We have some great people working within the system but we need to take on best management practices to enable the system to work better.

How would those you work with describe you?

I have been described as being driven, always putting the patient first, tolerant, perceptive, thoughtful and dedicated. My wife also says that I'm a bit idealistic and a bit of a dreamer, which I am. That is actually a good thing because it allows you to look at the big picture and the opportunities available, rather than focusing on the negative or small stuff.

What do you look for in those you work with?

I look for those who are great team players, good communicators, people who share my values, who are loyal, honest, flexible and who have a sense of fun. I look for those things because, ultimately, we're a team and we all have to try to work together on behalf of our patients. You're only as good as your weakest link and so we need our whole team to be on board. I certainly think that our front desk staff and administration team have a very challenging job at times. The people they deal with are sick or are worried that they are sick, so they are often not at their best when they're interacting with the front line. We try to value the contribution that all of our staff make and build on that.

What advice do you have for aspiring leaders?

Most importantly of all, I think you have to be passionate about what you do and about what you believe in. And don't get distracted. Research across the public and private sectors has shown that people can be very threatened by innovation and by change. And that has been evident in some of my experiences in healthcare. From time to time over the years, there have been obstacles put in my way to try and stop me from moving on or getting involved in different initiatives. And I have learnt that you just have to keep going. The world is not always fair. You have to be passionate about what you believe in and just continue to try and make yourself and your practice so good and inspiring to others that nothing can stop you.

How do you achieve innovation and improvement in your organisation?

Critical incident and process reviews

We do critical incident and process reviews in the practice. So, if something goes wrong or isn't working well, we don't scapegoat or blame. Instead, we try to look at the system and see what went wrong and what we need to do to fix it or make it better. I think that this systems approach to healthcare is missing throughout a lot of the health sector.

One example of how that has worked for us is with our phlebotomist.[3] About five years ago we were having a few bottleneck situations in the practice. At the time, we had four doctors and two nurses. It would be very busy in the mornings. Patients would see the doctor and then have to wait to see the nurse if they were to get blood tests done. The nurses were getting extremely busy because they often had their own appointments, dealing with dressings or baby vaccines and so on. So, on one hand, we were trying to provide a good service by offering blood tests on site. But, on the other hand, after seeing the doctor, people would then have to wait thirty or forty minutes to see the nurse. Some patients were getting a bit browned-off with that and, to be honest, I didn't blame them. It was a frustrating situation for everyone concerned. We decided there had to be a better way of doing things.

We decided to train up one of our secretaries to become a phlebotomist. She got some initial experience observing our nurse on site. Then she went and did a course in Cork and we also sent her to Galway and the Mater Hospital in Dublin. And then she went to Crumlin Hospital to learn how to take blood from babies. She became what I think was Ireland's first primary care phlebotomist about three years ago. So, now, anyone who wants a blood test books in with Róisín (the phlebotomist) in the mornings. That's done a number of things. First, it's providing a more timely user-friendly service for our patients from a person who is best trained, skilled and equipped to do that, which has led to the much smoother running of the practice. Second, it has freed up the nurses who can now concentrate on what they do best. Third, it has given a new career and enhanced job satisfaction to a valued team member. And, from a value point of view, there is a cost differential as well, in that patients who are on long-term medication can go to Róisín and pay €20 for that service, without having to see the doctor at all. So, there's a cost benefit there for the patient as well. Overall, we are giving people greater choice, we feel we are providing better efficiencies and we are getting people to do what they are best skilled to do.

---

[3] A person trained to draw blood.

The Waterford Health Park

We have always been multidisciplinary in focus and have tried to provide additional value for our patients. Historically, that involved bringing in extra services to the practice, such as physiotherapy and nurses. We built our own practice premises in 2001. A former mentor of mine had advised me to always plan for twice as much space as you think you will need. And so, when we built it we thought that we would never fill it. We had four thousand square feet and fourteen clinical rooms, even though we had only eight staff. Within two years, we were bursting at the seams because we brought in additional services and the practice grew organically. That experience made me realise that, if you were really to deliver on the potential of primary healthcare, things would have to be done very differently. So, I began to develop our concept and vision for the Waterford Health Park.

I began to read about best practice internationally and found out about the Bromley-by-Bow Centre in a deprived area of East London. I went to visit that with my architect. Now, I had no site or building at that stage, but we simply went on a fact-finding mission. I was totally amazed by what they were doing. They had developed a fantastic centre. They had one of the highest baby vaccination rates in Britain in an area where some of the large immigrant population didn't speak English. And I couldn't understand why this was. And it was really all because of innovation and thinking outside of the box. They had a huge appreciation of the value of art as part of a living health centre. So, they provided a free sketch for any mother and baby who came along for their six-week check at the baby clinic. Mothers were happy to come along and queue for an hour or two because they got a picture of their baby. And that really taught me a valuable lesson, which is, if you think outside the box, if you are innovative and if you're prepared to learn from best practice in other places, you can really add value to what you are trying to do yourself.

Then, about three years ago, the opportunity – or risk of a lifetime – came along. A beautiful old convent building came up for sale. It's a building of national importance and a protected structure. It was designed by Pugin, who was a famous architect in the 1840s. We decided to take it on and develop our Health Park there. We had no planning permission at the time. We needed to get special permission straight off to put up security cameras to protect the building. We then decided that the best way to achieve what we wanted to do was to get everybody on board and share our vision with them. We got a great team around us. We got a really good conservation architect who was passionate about old buildings. We brought all the local politicians up to the site and did up a model of what the project would look like when it was completed so that people could see what we were trying to do. And we tried to share our goal and our dream with as many people as possible. We invited down Duchas,[4] we contacted An Taisce[5] and we tried to engage with the local community as much as we could. And the results were great. We got no objections to our planning application. So, that side of things couldn't have gone better. We had a design team on site from January 2008 and the building was finished in May 2009.

The overall vision of the health park is to transform primary healthcare. It will focus on providing an enhanced range of services for people in their local community, including patient education, in a timely, efficient, cost-effective manner. We want our patients to view healthcare differently. We want them to view the facility as somewhere you can go to enjoy the surroundings. You might go into our internal courtyard garden to read or sit. You might go to a health talk or meditate in the beautiful Pugin Chapel. You might come in and have a cup of tea and a scone in the Pugin Café. It might be a way for you meet people. Or you might go to any of the many and varied health facilities on site. There is a general practice and a community pharmacy. In addition, we are the first HSE primary care team in Waterford, so we will have physiotherapists, occupational therapists, dietitians, domiciliary midwives, public health nurses, and speech and language therapists on site. We also have a counselling psychologist and some complementary therapy.

There is an operating theatre on site at the Waterford Health Park, which has the potential to allow for simpler day procedures to be done in the community, rather than in expensive hospital beds. We've future-proofed our facility in that regard.

Healthcare has to be about much more than the absence of disease. It's about helping people to feel well in themselves. That requires promoting

---

[4] Heritage service for Ireland.
[5] The National Trust for Ireland.

wellness rather than simply addressing illness. It also involves helping to bridge the huge gap that exists between what we know as doctors and nurses and what people on the street know. There's a huge gap. And that means that Irish men are dying, for example, five years younger than women. The average Irish man spends fifteen years of his life with a chronic illness, rates of many cancers continue to rocket and we have an epidemic of obesity and diabetes. I think, in the future, there will have to be much more crossover between health and education, not just in terms of research, which obviously is really important, but at a basic level. For instance, getting kids in primary school to exercise and eat healthy diets. And I think there's a great opportunity and potential for primary care to help bridge that gap. I think we need to be looking at health as much more than the health service or the Department of Health. Health is for all of us. It is our greatest asset. We must treasure it, but we must build on it and protect it as well.

There is another side to this development. I read this book called *Healthy Living Centres: A Guide to Primary Health Care Design* by Geoffrey Purves (Architectural Press, 2002) in which the author talks about the importance of 'the Wow factor'; the importance of putting a real signature building into your community, which can have a transforming affect by its physical presence, in terms of a feel-good factor and lifting the spirits. And that, ultimately, is what we want to do. We want to make a difference and to provide something for the community. We serve an underprivileged part of the city and I believe that, by putting a really beautiful building and quality services in place, we are really helping to improve health in the long term.

We commissioned the artist Jane O'Malley to provide us with some beautiful artworks for the atrium and waiting areas. Also, as part of our 'healing arts', the Omagh Peace Choir have performed a number of concerts in our atrium for our community, which has been a truly uplifting experience for everyone. This is all part of the new emerging paradigm in healthcare design called 'generative space'. This 'generative space' concept is where people's experience of a space fulfils the functional requirements but also improves their health, healthcare and quality of life. People should be able to articulate their experiences of the space in their own terms. Generative space is a newly emerging concept in the design of healthcare environments and leads to sustainable improvements over time. We hope to showcase generative space in our health park for our patients and families, staff, colleagues and our community. I believe it will lead to a new benchmark in healthcare delivery over time.

What examples do you have of encountering and overcoming difficulties?

Innovation as trial and error

Over the last couple of years, we've been trying to bring 'standard operating procedures' into the practice. We want to have a culture of doing things right the first time, every time. I'm not talking here about medical issues as such, although we meet regularly as clinicians to discuss clinical cases and learn from each other's experiences. I'm talking about the customer side of things such as making appointments, telephone skills, waiting times and so on. Initially, when we tried to bring in some changes there was some resistance from staff. Perhaps some people felt threatened about the level of performance and accountability associated with things being written down. Things went around in circles for a long time until we had to come up with a new approach, which was to look at our procedures from the inside out. In other words, when something goes wrong, say with an appointment, we try and look at that and see what happened and collectively learn from it in terms of what needs to change. And we have much more buy-in to that process now. But, of course, improvement is always ongoing.

How do you bring about change and what advice do you have for others about achieving change?

Change requires a team effort, so I'm a great believer in getting everybody around the table, clarifying what the goal is and then looking at what's going well and why, and what needs to improve and how. I always try and focus on what's positive. There are so many things that go well in healthcare, so it's important to recognise those before you focus on what you need to improve and change. Once we have received suggestions and come up with a solution, we tend to trial things for three months. After that, we review how it's gone and get feedback. If it turns out that something needs to be strengthened or changed, then we do it. Our general approach is that nothing is black and white and nothing is permanent. The only constant is change, as the saying goes. That's our general approach to achieving change. To make that approach work, having the right people around you is key. We always try and take on great people and build their confidence and their responsibilities. I'm a great believer in delegation and in giving people the responsibility and control to take over things themselves. I firmly believe that our people are our greatest asset and, if you harness all the talent and energy in your own team, you can do anything.

My advice to others bringing about change is to value everybody's contribution and to celebrate the small successes. It's important not to get negative and to focus on what's going well in addition to what needs to improve. Another useful principle in bringing about change is the SMART principle. This states that changes should be specific, measurable, realistic, time-framed and, most importantly, agreed. So you can't bulldoze change over people. You need to involve others in it. And remember that every journey begins with a single step. The direction of the journey is more important than the speed.

9

NUALA O'LOAN

Former police ombudsman for Northern Ireland; Ireland's roving
ambassador for conflict resolution; special envoy for Timor-Leste
(East Timor) and for women, peace and security; former Jean
Monnet Chair in European Law, University of Ulster

*Nuala O'Loan has held a variety of public sector leadership positions. Her lead-
ership career is grounded in strong personal beliefs and is characterised by an
emphasis on rights-based issues. She is particularly well known for her role as
police ombudsman for Northern Ireland, where she led investigations into the
police's handling of the Omagh bomb in 1998[1] and other controversial inquiries.
In December 2006, an independent survey by the Northern Ireland Statistics and
Research Agency found that Protestants and Catholics were equally supportive of
her office. In addition, a survey of police officers investigated by the Police
Ombudsman's Office suggested that 85 per cent believed they were treated fairly
by the office.*

---

[1] On Saturday, 15 August 1998 at 3.05 p.m., a terrorist bomb exploded in Omagh town,
Co. Tyrone, Northern Ireland. Twenty-nine people died and two hundred and fifty people
were injured, some seriously, as a result of the attack. The Police Ombudsman's report
on the investigation into the bomb states that it was 'the single worst terrorist incident
since the start of "The Troubles" in 1969'.

In recognition of her contribution to Northern Ireland, Nuala O'Loan was appointed Dame in December 2007. She also received a Person of the Year Award[2] in 2008 for her personal integrity and courage, her fearless commitment to the highest standards of policing for everyone in Northern Ireland and for her inspiring belief in justice and the rule of law as Northern Ireland's first police ombudsman. She was appointed to the House of Lords in 2009. Upon her appointment, she stated that she saw her new role as a wonderful opportunity, noting that throughout her career she has always tried to bring an independence of thought to issues in a way that would benefit people and enhance the services they receive.

Career Overview

I suppose that I have had a sort of curious career. I initially trained as a lawyer in London and then came to Northern Ireland where I was an academic in the University of Ulster. Then, quite early on, I became involved in rights-based issues – consumer rights and legal rights. I was given public appointments in a variety of areas, including energy, transport and general consumer rights. Then I went to Europe, to Brussels, where I worked as a legal expert in consumer matters. So, I have always worked in the field of people's rights and people's inability to access their rights. I was then appointed police ombudsman for Northern Ireland – to my great surprise – and it was on completion of that role that I was offered the job as special envoy for Timor-Leste.

What has motivated and directed you in the evolution of your career?

I think I was brought in the direction of rights-based issues by my very early experiences, which were quite difficult. My father died young and I was the eldest of eight children. We were very poor and I was acutely conscious of the difficulties associated with that. Later, as a young student working in a law centre as a volunteer, I became aware that such difficulties were global. I also became aware that the inability to get what you should

---

[2] The Person of the Year Awards are organised annually by the Rehab Group and televised by RTÉ.

be entitled to, and even sometimes to articulate your problem, was something with which I could deal.

In terms of what motivates and drives me, I think I have some kind of passionate commitment to justice. I have this feeling that we are actually only here for a short time and that each of us has the ability to make a difference; that there are hugely different ways by which we can contribute and that we should use as much as we can of the opportunities that life presents. I think it's that that drives me above all. I've also got a strong faith and I think that drives me because I remember, as an eighteen-year-old, learning from the prophet Michael that the Lord asks that you act justly, that you love tenderly and that you walk humbly with your God.

I think you can ask questions about what spirituality is. But fundamentally leadership is about people. People to me are whole beings – they are physical, they are intellectual and they are also spiritual. The whole person has to be cared for and valued and has huge potential when this is the case. So, I think that there is a large place for spirituality in leadership. I think, too, that it has enabled me in the most difficult of circumstances to say, 'This isn't about me' so I don't need to think about me. This is about what I am trying to achieve. And it had better be right. So, together my commitment to justice and my faith are strong motivating forces.

What does leadership mean to you?

I think, in part, leadership is the ability to inspire people and to enable people so that they can help you to achieve your objectives. My leadership roles have all involved others. So, it's not that you are a solitary being that charges away into the horizon. Really, you bring with you a team and the teams get bigger and bigger. Leadership emerges in the motivating of the team. Then, and this was particularly important in the context of the role of police ombudsman, you have to engage all of the other players in the context in which you operate. They have to be prepared to take ownership of some part of what you are delivering in service terms.

So, for me, leadership means the ability to inspire and to enable people to deliver something that I want to achieve. Leadership also means having a vision which I can communicate, it means enabling others to understand the wisdom of the vision and to amend the vision if I haven't got it right. That means being a listening leader and an inclusive leader. Leadership is about having the clarity of purpose that enables people to understand what I want them to do, why they should do it and how they should do it. I think that, in public service delivery, leadership is all about how you do it. And it's about modelling the kind of behaviour that you expect people to have. As a result, I think that leadership must be very people oriented.

I view management as a process which enables leadership. I'm not a technical expert in these matters but, as I consider the various situations in which I find myself, management is necessary to ensure that things happen. It doesn't really matter if the things in question are the forensic examination of a scene or the delivery of a package of items to Timor so that we can take matters forward there, or – the process in which I am currently involved – interviewing members of parliament in England and Wales about the human rights enquiry. Management is what enables those things to happen. Leadership is about the articulation of vision, purpose and strategy, which are then delivered through management.

My own leadership style is direct, robust and inclusive. I challenge a lot. I can remember, in my early days as police ombudsman, when people would come to me with a problem. I would sit back and I would ask them what my options were. They would then typically say, 'But that's why I came to you.' When that happened I would have to remind them that they were a skilled person facing a problem in their specialist area. I'd ask them to think about it and come back to me, and then we'd talk about it. I took that approach because leadership is about enabling people to develop. If they develop they are more committed and if they are more committed they'll be happier and they'll produce a better product.

I also do walkabout very often. And that is a very solid part of my leadership. I think it's very important, because you can pick up the little things that can cause an organisation to become dysfunctional. In fact, you can pick them up quite early. When I do see something, I then ask the manager or director of the area to address the issue. You don't have to interfere yourself. You can leave management to those responsible for management, while still maintaining a leadership role.

What has shaped you as a leader?

That's a difficult question. As I mentioned earlier, I'm the eldest of eight children and my father died early. That meant that I had a very difficult childhood. I assumed a sort of leadership role in the family. However, in terms of real leadership, in organisational terms, my experiences as police ombudsman really shaped me. I had to learn that it was alright to be afraid as a leader. But I had to deal with the fear. For example, after my Omagh bomb report,[3] which was regarded as very contentious, a lot of angry things were said about me. So, there was a huge, huge media flurry around me for a couple of weeks. And I had made a decision that I would say what I had to say and I would not then engage further. Because, once I had made my report, it was then for the police to start investigating the Omagh bomb again. Then, having made that decision and having listened to the nonsense that was being said about me, I wanted to come out and correct the inaccuracies. But my colleagues counselled me and said, 'No, you decided you're not going to do that. You decided you're not going to speak.' Once I had accepted that, I can remember thinking to myself, 'So, if I can't go and rebut these errors then I'd better go and buy a sandwich' and then thinking, 'What'll happen if I'd go and buy a sandwich? Is somebody going to attack me?' And then finally I thought that if I couldn't go and buy a sandwich then I couldn't be police ombudsman, so I had better get on with it. So, there is something about making yourself operate as well.

How would those who work with you describe you?

I know how people describe me because they have told me. They can be very complimentary. People like being cared for. They actually like feeling like human beings, being respected and being treated as if their dignity matters. I'm a hands-on person. And people have to learn to live with that. For example, in the work I was doing as police ombudsman, it was absolutely vital that I knew about everything I was talking about. In order

---

[3] The Omagh bomb report was undertaken under the provisions of the Police (Northern Ireland) Act 1998 (the Police Act), Section 55(6)(b). This states that the Police Ombudsman for Northern Ireland may, without a complaint, formally investigate a matter in accordance with Section 56 of the Act, if it is desirable in the public interest.

to know it, I had to absorb it. And, in order to absorb it, I had to read all the statements, check all the forensics reports and all that. Staff who weren't accustomed to that level of intrusion would produce a report and perhaps expect that report to be there and that to be it. They perhaps found my way of working a little difficult. But it enabled me to function. I could then stand in front of the world and say, 'This is true. And I have done enough work to know that it is true.'

What, in your opinion, are the characteristics of effective leaders?

I think effective leaders are clear and they have a purpose. That is one thing. And they have communication skills, which I think are critically important. I think a really effective leader can engage a number of different types of audience. So, for example, in my role as police ombudsman I had a police audience, a technical audience, a public audience – which was the ordinary audience – and I had politicians and broader non-government organisation (NGO) stakeholders who operated in the criminal justice field.

Sometimes, as a leader, you actually have to face angry people. I experienced that in a difficult situation in a community where there had been an interface problem. One side of the community was very hostile and I went up to meet them because of various things that had happened. I can remember going into the hall and facing these two hundred or so people who were angry with me, angry that things weren't going the way they would have liked. But my experience always was that, if you were honest with them, if you were frank insofar as you could – because there were things that you couldn't always say – they would respect you for that. And that you would make some sort of accommodation with them. I never left a meeting feeling that I had to leave or that there was a bad taste about the meeting. It was never like that. We always managed to get somewhere.

I can also think of when I have had to stand in front of and speak to very angry police officers. In particular, I can think of an occasion when police officers were sent into Stormont to search an administrative office. I think there were twenty-four officers who went up and down the steps of Stormont. Somebody alleged that they had been assaulted by one of those officers. We had to identify that officer. But I was required by law to notify each of them that they may be the suspect. So, the letters went out. And I got, I think, a dozen angry letters, which I gave to my senior director and said, 'You deal with the letters.' And I said to my secretary, 'Will you ring them up and tell them that I am coming down to see them.' Because it seemed to me that, if they were as angry as all that, I needed to get in and we needed to have a proper conversation about it. A series of telephone calls took place and it became evident that they didn't want me to come. They were very angry and they didn't want to meet me. But my secretary understood that that was not an issue. So, it was arranged for just a couple of days later.

I remember going down to this bleak, dark police station, and the armoured Land Rovers outside, the queues of them. The officers were standing waiting for me in their riot gear, big, tall fellows with their arms folded. And I stepped out of my little car, on my own, feeling the anger. I knew that I had to do it. I knew I had to go. And I knew that, once I talked to them – because they were professional people – that they would understand that the notices were served for their benefit. So that the officer who had committed the offence could defend himself or herself. If they weren't the officer, then they had nothing to worry about. And it took about a ten-minute conversation standing there in the station yard. Then we all got in the Land Rover and away we went. And we had a very enjoyable and interesting evening – out on patrol.

So, overall, I think effective leaders have the ability to have a very clear strategy and to articulate that strategy. I think leadership is about both the public face of the leader and having systems, processes and quality assurance mechanisms which ensure that things happen as they should. In the police ombudsman's office, one of our biggest things during the year was not just business planning, but our quarterly review of where we had got to on the targets. Did we need to shift resources? Were some people working too hard? Were some people not working hard enough? So, there was a constant oversight of the whole process. Then, at the end of the year came the evaluation and the celebration.

What do you look for in those you work with and what advice do you have for aspiring leaders?

I look for loyalty, commitment, flexibility and people who can really pull out the stops when I need them to be pulled out. And the loyalty that I look for is not just loyalty to the organisation, but loyalty to their colleagues. But I also look for honesty. If there are things wrong, I want to know about them: I want the whistle-blowers. And then I look for technical skill, because we all need technical skills. I also look for accuracy and attention to detail, because a lot of the work that I do is around evidence-based decision-making. So, I think that I demand an awful lot from people.

In terms of advice to aspiring leaders, I would say work very hard. Be prepared to work harder than anybody else. Be honest. Give of yourself. Don't hold yourself back. Don't think that leadership is about being distant, because I don't think it is. Be prepared to engage when things are difficult. Don't run away. Be prepared to say that you got it wrong. And that's probably enough advice.

Achieving innovation and improvement in organisations: what examples do you have from the front line?

We came to the job of setting up the police ombudsman's office with nothing; we didn't even have paper clips. That gave us the advantage of designing the structure within which people would work. The physical structure was designed so that you had interaction and people had the opportunity to learn from each other. We had tables divided into four, with four people sitting around each. We also had specialist units with a lot of high security around some of their work. But, for me, I think the thing that worked particularly well was the core process which we established, which was the process of investigation. We had to work out what an investigation should look like and how it should be done. So, for example, if you have to arrest a police officer, you don't have to go at six o'clock in the morning; there may be other ways of doing it.

Of course, it wasn't always right and in such instances we had to go back and rewrite the policies and guidance for the staff. Then, after a big enquiry, we would always go back and revisit it and try to work out what had happened, because the process was core. I always said to staff that, by their actions and by my actions, our integrity and our reputation would be either safeguarded or damaged. And that's a huge burden to carry every day.

The reality was that there were people who wanted us to fail. And there were people who would have been delighted had we failed. And it was critical that we didn't fail. If we couldn't fail then we had to get it right. So, we didn't have the opportunity to make big mistakes. We had the opportunity for small mistakes, but not big mistakes. Setting up that process of investigation was core. We had delegations from all over the world who came to see what we had done and what was different about it. I was interested because when the Garda Ombudsman Commission and the Independent Police Complaints Commission of England and Wales came along to see how we had done it, they had existing investigation experience available to them. And the difference actually lay in the finer details rather than in the, you know, you send people out, you knock on doors. But it's how you knock on the door. It's about how you are dressed when you knock on the door. It's about how you respond. It's about whether you think about what the person says to you and then think, 'What else should I be asking them? Is there anything else that comes specifically from this?' You send people out with the list of questions, yes. But they always have this flexibility. I think those are the things that made it a successful process. And it was.

What examples do you have of encountering and overcoming difficulties?

One difficulty I encountered was that I tried to introduce mediation into police complaints. Mediation is a process by which two parties agree that they will meet together to try to resolve something in a way which is, in police complaints terms, simpler. When complaints occurred, we had either an investigation or what was called informal resolution. Informal resolution was a process by which the police officer and the complainant were asked what had happened. Then there was an attempt to explain to the complainant what had happened and an attempt to resolve the issue. But it did not satisfy complainants, usually. So, I wanted to be able to mediate. I wanted to sit both parties down in the same room – as I had seen done in the States and other places. It would be much quicker than investigating, in these simpler cases. Very often, you don't have the evidence; you don't have witnesses or things like that for cases of, for example, somebody being very rude to somebody else. So, it would have been quicker and simpler. It would have been cheaper. It would have saved the police officer under investigation a lot of worry; it would have saved their families the worry.

Everything was there to confirm that this was a good process. But the Police Federation for Northern Ireland wouldn't go for it. And I think it was all around the objection which did exist at the very top of the Police Federation to me. Because I set in train the processes repeatedly. I trained mediators and all that sort of thing. At the last minute they would pull back and say, 'No, we're not ready, we're not ready yet.' And, as soon as I had gone, mediation was up and running. And that's not a good thing.

I'm not sure that it would have been possible to approach the Federation in any different way because the Federation are the union for the police officers and the central council, the leading part of the Federation, would never meet me from the day I was appointed. So, in a way, it was never how I conducted the office, it was simply that I was the police ombudsman. And they didn't want me. They would never meet me. I met their committees and some things like that. But, as soon as my successor went in, the central committee met him. I think that it was just a difficulty I had to manage. The triumph for me, of course, was that, by the time I left, we would anonymously survey all officers who had been investigated. We had investigated thousands. And I think 90 per cent said they thought it was fair. So we had achieved with the ordinary officers, if not with the union.

When I do have disappointments I deal with them by trying to get on to the next thing. But, first, I do try and work out why things didn't work, see if I could have done it differently and whether there is some change that I can make in the future to ensure that whatever has caused the disappointment doesn't recur. And then I get on with the next thing. There is no point in dwelling on it.

So, how do you bring about change?

I think it's massively difficult to bring about change. Change is the product of a number of different structures and processes. It needs leadership and it needs management as well. And it's facile to say it, but people need to understand what is going to happen and why it's going to happen. They need to be signed up to the process of change. All those things together can be hugely difficult and hugely challenging, because change threatens people where they are comfortable. The reality, of course, is that an organisation that doesn't change is an organisation that is moribund. The context in which it operates will change constantly. I think that, really, it is essential that you put those things together; that you put processes in and check what's happening. Keep coming back to this checking. If people agree to change, if they sign up to change and you introduce change in a measured and mannered way and it's what they expect, the impact of it can still be something they don't expect. Therefore, sometimes that has to be explored and sometimes there has to be slight modifications to what you are proposing to do. But, at the end of the day, everybody has to – or as many as possible – have to sign up. In any organisation there will always be malcontents who simply won't agree, but I find that persuasion involves listening to people and having them involved in creating the vision in the first instance; having them involved in setting the targets that will enable the achievement of the vision.

Maintaining support for a vision also requires being with people in their tough times and acknowledging that they'll get things wrong. When people get things wrong, one of the things I always say is, 'Whatever happens, I am behind you.' So if, for example, you get something horrendously wrong, it's my fault. Because I'm providing this service and it's my responsibility. So, come and tell me about it. And we can work out why it happened and we can move the change further on.

Overall, I think achieving change is all about respecting people. I also think that the reality is that all these other people with whom I'm working probably have far more valuable ideas about change than me, because they are there working at the coalface and can see where efficiencies can be created. So, listening to people, thinking about what they have to say and letting them talk to each other from their different perspectives enables a complete understanding of the process of the business. And that helps you to get your change right.

What have been your key learning points?

One of my key learning points was learning to communicate, which I think I really cracked as chair of the electricity council. The brief there was enormously technical so I had to communicate something in a field in which I was not comfortable. But I learnt to do that. And that taught me that attention to detail was the key – a very important lesson for the role of police ombudsman. The whole process of being police ombudsman meant that every day was a learning moment. There, I learnt resilience, I learnt to step back and I learnt detachment. The other key thing I learnt was that, if people had come to me, for example, to look for an investigation into a murder, I had to learn to place my emotions to one side. Your emotions are important because they make you a human being, but I had to learn to place them to one side and be utterly professional; to be compassionate to people while thinking, 'What can I do? What are the options? Are there investigative opportunities here? Can I give these people something?' Did I have to say to them then, 'There is nothing I can do to help you, I'm very sorry' or would I tell them that there were possibilities and maybe we could help them. So, I learnt that I had to put myself out of the picture and that I didn't matter. I could go home and cry afterwards, but my tears were of no value to them. That was a big learning experience.

Another large piece of learning came from one of the simplest experiences that I had. I wanted to set up an office that was impartial and that was very respectful of people. When we were doing our initial six weeks of training, we spent a week on 'Who am I?', 'What baggage do I bring to this office?' and 'What biases do I have?' Because we all have biases and we all have baggage. The idea was that, if you could identify your baggage and your biases, you could deal with them in a way that wouldn't impact on others. This took place in late October and I had sixty odd people in a room. We were talking about how we would do business and the question which arose was, 'Can we wear a poppy?' It was such a simple question but, at the same time, very loaded. There are organisations which have said, 'Nobody can wear a poppy' and they have problems. And there are organisations where they say, 'You can wear a poppy if you want to' and they have problems. They all looked at me. I remember thinking, well, if they can't sort out whether we can wear a poppy or not, we're not going to be able to run this office. So, I sat back and I said, 'No. You work it out for yourselves. What are we going to do about this?' And it was setting the policy really. And it went round and round and it got tenser and tenser. And I began to think, I'm losing them, I'm losing them. And I thought, well, if you're losing them you really don't belong here anyway. So, I wanted to rescue it. And I was encouraged by others to try to facilitate it rather than rescue it.

Eventually they got there and found a solution that they all signed up to. They came to the conclusion that, so long as it wouldn't offend others in the team in which they were working, they could wear the poppy if they wanted to. And that those on the team would recognise what the poppy meant to them. That if they were going to certain districts that they would not wear a poppy, because it would be regarded as indicative of a whole lot of allegiances which would not be impartial, or not be perceived to be impartial. So, there were occasions when it was permissible and there were occasions when it wasn't. The ultimate thing was that we respected each other and the things that are precious to people. And it worked. For several years we had no problems in that regard. But there could have been massive dysfunction in the office because of that.

What advice do you have for others who would like to bring about change?

My advice to others would be to be careful and don't jump into change. Work out exactly what it is you want to do and why you want to do it. And then work out with staff how it might get done. Work out the critical factors that will enable what it is that you want to do. And figure out how you can achieve those critical factors that will bring about the greater change that you are seeking. Finally, listen to those you are working with, particularly when things are getting difficult and tense.

10

KENNETH MCDONALD

**Consultant cardiologist at St Vincent's University Hospital; director
of the Heart Failure Unit at St Vincent's University Hospital;
professor of Medicine at University College Dublin (UCD); director
of the Heartbeat Trust**

*Kenneth McDonald is a consultant cardiologist at St Vincent's University Hospital,
where he is the director of the Heart Failure Unit. In addition, he is medical director of the Heart Beat Trust. Launched in 2005, this organisation supports research
and special services in the Heart Failure Unit in St Vincent's University Hospital
Group. The main foci of the charity are to raise public awareness of the risk of
developing cardiomyopathy and heart failure; to develop improved strategies for
detecting cardiomyopathy earlier in its development and preventing its progression
to heart failure; and to enhance collaborative management between the commu-
nity- and hospital-based services of both people with and those at risk of
developing cardiomyopathy and heart failure.*

Career overview: evolution and motivation

I qualified in Medicine in 1981. I studied in UCD and did most of my
undergraduate work at St Vincent's Hospital. I then spent one year at St

James's Hospital in Dublin before going abroad to the US, where I was based at the University of Minnesota for ten years. In my first three years there, I focused on gaining additional training. Then, in 1991, I went on the staff of the University of Minnesota Hospital and Clinics, at the University of Minnesota. It was a great place to be, an enjoyable place to live and everything was going well. In fact, at that stage of my career I thought that I was going to remain there. Then my wife, who is also a doctor, was offered a post in Tallaght Hospital. As a result, my choice was either to come back to Dublin or to have a transatlantic marriage. Unsurprisingly, I returned to Dublin in 1998, to work in cardiology at St Vincent's Hospital.

I came back to work in the area of heart failure, which was one of my areas of interest. My colleague and mentor at St Vincent's, Dr Brian Maurer, had always wanted to develop that area of the hospital. So, when I came back, my plan was to try to develop heart failure services, as well as to undertake my other necessary duties as a cardiologist.

I think what drives and motivates me in my clinical and service development endeavours is almost a cliché – making people feel better is an enjoyable thing to do. Nonetheless, it remains true for the overriding majority of doctors. I am very fortunate to work in something that I like to do. I suppose it's the same for life in general – it's nice to do things that you find productive and enjoyable and that are also of some help to those around you.

What does leadership mean to you?

For me, leadership entails being able to stand back, to see what's needed, to decide how best to achieve it and to identify who you need around you to accomplish it. That process should involve leaders taking account of the multiple opinions about what we should be doing. Once a course of action has been decided, a leader must then decide how best to achieve it. Of course, getting anything done is obviously going to be a team effort.

In the health service I think that we are currently lacking both a wide perspective on what we should be doing and a clear view of how we can achieve that. I don't believe that this country has ever had that initial debate about what society wants from healthcare; we have never asked ourselves whether we should focus on primary care, keeping people well, or whether we want to focus on having the ultimate in healthcare through hospitals.

So, I think that wider debate has to occur. The outcomes of that debate can then inform policy choices and provide a framework by which decisions about resource allocation can be made.

If I was to describe what I do as a leader, I would say that my approach is to delegate to safe hands. I like to have people working with me who know what we are trying to do and who share the big-picture view that I hold. When such people are in place, they tend to take responsibility for an area and I don't really have to worry too much about it because they have the same vision, drive and enthusiasm as me. As a result, I know they are going to work hard and get on with the task at hand. In effect, this means that I can adopt a laissez-faire approach with my core team. I definitely don't micromanage and I don't look at every detail of what my team do. There are, of course, pluses and minuses to my approach. However, it works for me, in significant part because I am fortunate to have very, very good people who work with me.

What has shaped you as a leader?

The people that I have worked with have influenced me greatly. They have influenced both the direction my career has taken and the way that I work. I think that must be true of everyone who takes on any form of leadership role: you are brought there by the people you have worked with. I think that, even if you haven't perceived those individuals as wonderful leaders, you are probably still influenced by their personality or modus operandi.

For me, within the area of heart failure, I had the seed of interest sown in my brain by Dr Brian Maurer. He is my senior colleague, who I worked with a lot with over the years. My interest in heart failure meant that I made sure I worked in a hospital which was renowned in that area. In the University of Minnesota the chief I worked under was extraordinarily dedicated. In my experience, working with someone who is dedicated to your cause cultivates and encourages your interest.

My personality has also strongly shaped my approach to getting things done. No matter what aspect of life I am dealing with, even if it's opening an electronic gadget, I don't read the rules. I plug it in and get on with it. I think that there is good and bad to that. The good aspect of it is that you make a start, even if it's not perfect. Nonetheless, I am aware that if you step back and read a little about what you are going to do, and try and take the advice of others who have done it before, you probably can get things done more effectively. I tend to dive in and learn as I do things.

How would those who work with you describe you?

I think how people see me depends on their perspective: whether they are based within or outside of my service. I think that those I have worked with in developing my service would probably say that I delegate; that I look at the big picture; that I am not necessarily very attentive to detail; and that I get frustrated when I don't see things moving forward. I also get frustrated when I'm working with people who don't have or share my drive and enthusiasm for the area of heart failure. People might also say that I try to cultivate those who are of a similar mind to me. The corollary of that is that I try to move those who are not to the side, even though they may be effective as individuals. As a result, although it has never been said to me directly, those who have never been of the same mind as me may say that I am far too focused on my own area and insufficiently tolerant of others.

What do you look for in the people you are working with?

In the area of heart failure I look for absolute single-minded dedication to the area. It is an area which has suffered from lack of attention. That's not a criticism of anyone or any body in the past, because it is a criticism you could direct to anywhere around the world. It has never been a condition which people have had the time or the resources to deal with, so I look for other people who might realise that this is something that needs to be nurtured, cultivated and sustained. We haven't yet got it to the point where it has its own natural momentum. But thankfully there are a lot of people, not just in our unit but also emerging throughout the country, who see this as important.

What do you think are the characteristics of effective leaders in healthcare and hospitals?

Medicine is bedeviled by politics between the groups that are involved. There are too many people who fight for their own ends without seeing the big picture. People accuse me of that and may say that I defend the heart failure patient and service to the exclusion of other equally important things. Now, that may be the case, but it makes the need for someone who looks at the big picture of the healthcare service all the greater. And, as I have mentioned, I don't think that there is yet a clear view at the top in terms of what we want from our health service. Answering that question is not going to be achieved in a week's review of the situation. It is as fundamental a decision as the type of infrastructure that you put in place in a country. You don't just go out and build a road without knowing where the road leads. Similarly, you shouldn't be developing a healthcare service in a piecemeal fashion.

When I think of leadership in hospitals I recognise that, within the structure of a hospital, the goals of management are not the same as the goals of the healthcare providers. That is a critical obstruction to the optimal working of any unit. Put more bluntly, the managers and the doctors, the managers and the nurses, the managers and the healthcare professionals may not have the same goals. Mangers are looking at budgetary issues and the budgetary mechanisms of the health service are very dated. They work with a year-on-year budget, without planning over a longer time frame. In contrast, clinicians tend to be focused on developing optimal services, often without thinking of budget. The latter is a criticism of clinicians, but the key point is that managers and clinicians don't necessarily gel very easily. There are daily annoyances and different foci. If a manager was writing this, I am sure that they might consider giving out about the waywardness of consultants, doctors and nurses who don't see the cost of things. There would be some substance to that criticism as well, because those factors haven't been part and parcel of our education.

One area that healthcare leaders can be effective in, in the current climate, is moving responsibility for health to the individual. I sometimes get the sense from the healthcare debates in this country that healthcare delivery is seen as the responsibility of the Department of Health, the Health Service Executive (HSE), the local hospital and the general practitioner (GP), rather than the responsibility of the individual. I think we need to change that so that the individual realises that the initial responsibility lies with them. Of course, people also have the right to demand that they are getting good community and hospital services and that their politicians and the HSE are ensuring that healthcare delivery is formulated correctly. Improvements in health service delivery won't happen overnight. But there are things we can all do as individuals to improve our healthcare – literally overnight.

What advice do you have for aspiring leaders in hospitals?

My advice for aspiring physicians would be to become more skilled in management. I think that is important. People of my age bracket haven't got specific training in this area, so we can fly by the seat of our pants on occasion. Taking management skills on board would probably harmonise the relationships we have with management in hospitals. Trying to create a hybrid individual who would be very skilled in both medicine and management may be difficult, but they are attempting to do that at present by trying to get consultants to take on more of the clinical-managerial role. I think that the ability to make significant managerial decisions will be required to make those roles meaningful. I also think there is some scepticism as to how much power a clinical manager will have in practice – as opposed to being the fall guy if things don't go well.

What examples do you have of innovation in action?

Development of the Heart Failure Unit in St Vincent's Hospital

If you spend money on a heart failure service you are going to keep people out of hospital. Heart failure is a chronic disease and we should be monitoring it selectively in the community with very little hospital involvement. That's what we are trying to impress on people. If you do that you save lives by giving people a better quality of life and you save financially as you minimise the need for emergency-room visits. That's the clinical service we're working towards. But it is important to couple that with the research end of things. The Heart Failure Unit and research staff in UCD, supported by the Heartbeat Trust, are doing a lot of clinical, basic and service-delivery research work, because there is a lot about the disease which is still unknown. We have some very effective research people who are helping us to tease that out and who are feeding that information back to us. We are linking in with them on a weekly basis.

I think my achievements in heart failure have been helped by my coming in with the right interest at the right time in the right environment. There was an awful lot to be gained from putting a proper structure and service in place in the area of heart failure. There were benefits for patients through improvements in their quality of life and there were also financial benefits, because it did lead to a lot of financial savings. The service developed in St Vincent's because I was interested in it and I got the support that I required from management and my colleagues within the hospital. We also quickly and effectively managed to show the improvement in quality of life for patients. Those results were recognised internationally and helped us to become known as a leading international unit for our work on restructuring how heart failure should be cared for. That took a long time to achieve, but we were lucky to have the tide with us in what we wanted to do.

Getting space and funding for the unit were critical practicalities and would never have happened if a couple of crucial people hadn't worked with me. One such individual – now a member of the heart failure service – was an employee of a pharmaceutical company. He came up to my office and said that he had some money to do a heart failure survey. We got chatting and were like minded, and he offered to talk to me if there were greater opportunities for support from his company. He managed to get us some seed money from them, which allowed us to get additional staff and space. The service is now officially operating for ten years and is, in part, sponsored by the HSE. It is also supported by the Heartbeat Trust, which is a charitable organisation which we set up to fund the service. It is a continual battle to try and maintain the resources, and I imagine next year and the year after are going to be even more difficult for us.

Despite the fact that the HSE receives a lot of criticism, I do have to emphasise that they worked well with us. When I asked for support, they asked for proof that the service worked. The cynic would say they want you to go off and do the work and when you have proven yourself, they will come in, take the credit for it and roll the service out. I wouldn't look at it that way. I think they just challenged us to go out and do the job. And each time we come to a critical point in the service, we go back to the HSE and say that we have proven this now, that it improves quality of life, saves money and the HSE should take this on. And they are taking it on, although not as quickly as I would like. In the last couple of years they have formed a number of working groups in the area. That is a very positive development. There are some very effective people in those working groups who will try and bring the area forward.

What is your approach to achieving change?

In terms of achieving change, I have learnt the value of being single-minded and focused; the benefit of getting good supportive data to hound people with; and the advantage of the nuclear option of highlighting to the public that they are not getting the service they should be getting. This latter option is really only viable if you know that what you are saying is objectively and factually correct. At the end of the day, we have responsibilities as doctors and healthcare providers to all of the people that we work for: the HSE, the Department of Health and our own hospital, as well as the patient. As a result, I strongly prefer to work in a collaborative fashion by showing people the reasons why a service is needed and should be developed. I think it is also useful to highlight the benefits which will accrue for everyone, even the managers of healthcare services, if they are seen to be the people pushing something forward. So, there is the selfishness factor for all of us involved. But if the collegial collaborative approach isn't working, then I do believe that we have an obligation to take less collaborative and even confrontational approaches to get the message across.

What advice do you have for others attempting to bring about change in the health service?

I don't think that it's ever been easy to achieve change in any healthcare service. However, we are going to face a particularly rocky road over the next couple of years as funding is tight. In this country, I think the fundamental challenges are taking the politics out of healthcare and ensuring personal accountability. I think healthcare has tended to be dominated by decisions that have high visibility. Politicians have tended to be interested in things which facilitate good public relations, rather than things that are important foundations for good healthcare delivery, but won't grab headlines or won't be finished during their tenure in the job.

The country is heading into severe financial constraints over the next couple of years and it will be very difficult to move anything forward. In those circumstances, the challenge is to be more innovative. I would say to people that the first thing they have to ensure is that their idea can stand up to objective scrutiny. It will also help if the initiative is relevant to a wide sector of the population. If that is the case, you should get a large number of like-minded people together and get them to push a coherent message out there, in a collaborative way. I would suggest this because I think that having the same message on heart failure coming out from a small number of people in St Vincent's has probably numbed the message a little bit. I think if we had a wider group of people delivering the same message that we would have pushed things forward a lot quicker.

11

BEN DUNNE

**Entrepreneur; CEO of Ben Dunne Fitness Group; CEO of the
Nora Dunne Gallery; columnist with the *Irish Sun***

Ben Dunne is CEO of the Ben Dunne Fitness Group, which runs three fitness centres in the Dublin area - Carlisle, Westpoint and Northwood. The development of the chain is ongoing. He has also recently opened the Nora Dunne Art Gallery in the grounds of one of his fitness centres. The gallery charges a much lower commission charge than the industry average, with the aim of opening up the market to more Irish artists. Previously, Ben Dunne's investment focus was on property and retail portfolios. He is a former director of Dunnes Stores, one of the largest department store chains in Ireland. He worked his way through the ranks to accede his father as director. In 1981, he was kidnapped by the IRA and held for seven days.

Career overview and evolution

Arriving at the place I am today has been an incredible journey and is quite a story. Although I have successfully built my own business, for a time, I would have been unemployable elsewhere. Almost nineteen years ago I had some well-documented difficulties with drug abuse and drug addiction. As a result of those, I lost my job in Dunnes Stores. Unsurprisingly, I then hit rock bottom. But I am resilient and that is a very valuable trait. So I started out again and went into the health and fitness business. That took a lot of courage, really. I had been fired from Dunnes Stores because of my personal issues and then, very shortly afterwards, I started a new business. That is always demanding, both personally and professionally. But the decision to start the new business was nearly made for me because I had nothing to do. I had been running one of the largest companies in Ireland and then found myself out of a job. Unfortunately that's the situation that a lot of people are finding themselves in now. For me, it was never life threatening and I was never going to starve, but having a job does give you a focus and a sense of purpose. Thankfully, I have good brain that I wanted to keep active and that drove me to become involved in the health and fitness business. Although I obviously drew on my prior business experience, my success at building that business was an example of just how much you can achieve with determination – and a little bit of luck. Now that the business is established, the thing that keeps me engaged and wanting to develop it further is knowledge. I keep myself informed about the business I am in, the latest developments and the things that are no longer up-to-date or of value. Keeping informed in that way is what allows you to lead your organisation in the right direction.

There are lots of things involved in my current work of sustaining and building the Ben Dunne Fitness Group. But the main things that I deal with on a day-to-day basis are people related. Once you have a clear sense of what you want to achieve in a business, the focus shifts to getting it done – and that all happens through people. In my case, it's the people who work in my business and the people who use the clubs. I think it's very important that my employees are getting job satisfaction and that just doesn't happen of its own accord. Anybody can bring the worst out in people, but it takes a lot of talent, effort and patience to bring the best out in people. You can develop people if you work with them – even people who mightn't be the best team players. As a result of our willingness to do that, people who mightn't have made it in other organisations have progressed well working for the Ben Dunne Fitness Group.

What does leadership mean to you?

Good leadership means that you set the direction and pace for your organisation. And if you are a really good leader, people can push you even further than you want to go. That happens because people work hard for people and things they believe in, and they like to have a role in success. If they are interested and believe in what you are trying to do, they help to push it forward. Because of that dynamic, I think that people should enjoy good leadership. They should be enthused by the direction and goals that you have set and their involvement in achieving them.

For me, you can learn a lot about good leadership from sport. People like playing on a team with a good captain: they work towards a clear goal and help each other to score points for the team. The other lesson for leadership from sport is that you can be friendly with your captain, but while you're on duty you've got to respect them. My own philosophy about being a leader is that, although people should respect you, if you earn the points you don't have to be referred to as 'Mister' or 'The Boss' or your title. So, in my opinion, good leadership is all about setting a clear goal for the team to achieve, and helping to create an environment in which everyone helps to earn points for the rest of the team. I think that there are lots of ways you can do that, but the key thing is that it's easy to know whether people are receiving good leadership. You'll see it in the job satisfaction of staff and in their enjoyment of working in the organisation. You'll see it in the amount of sick days, in staff turnover and the bottom line. You'll also see it when there's need for an extra effort and whether people give that willingly. There really are so many indicators that show whether an organisation is being well led. One less formal indicator of whether your leadership is effective is whether people do anything differently when you are on or off the premises. It definitely shouldn't be the case that people say, 'The boss is coming and we have to tidy up today.' Bad leadership can be seen when there are two standards in a business: one when the boss is in head office and one when he is not around. There should be the same commitment and standards whether the leader is on the premises or not. In politics you can measure leadership by votes – and in business it's nearly as simple.

My own leadership style isn't conventional. I don't believe that accountants or people in the law industry should play a huge role in the running of certain types of business. My leadership is based on knowing a lot about the business that I'm in. If you don't know about your business, you're going to end up in trouble. And one thing about the present recession is that it's going to show up weakly run companies very quickly. My leadership is also based on selecting and supporting the people on my team. You just can't take somebody who doesn't have an interest in medicine or business and make them into a good doctor or business person. So, good leadership also needs to be accompanied by astuteness in selecting people – to make sure that they have the ability and the interest to do the job. If you could teach people to do things, the world would be full of people like Tiger Woods. So, while you can develop people's talents, they have to have a natural love for what they're doing. And if people really like what they're doing, there's huge room for development.

Overall, then, for me, good leadership is about setting a direction, selecting the right people to help you get there, supporting them so that they can achieve their goals, and seeing results in the day-to-day running of the business and on the bottom line.

What has shaped you as a leader?

I went through a period of hopeless failure in my life. Thankfully, I did learn an awful lot from that experience. That learning came from analysis and reflection about why I hit that failure period. I learnt that my problems all started with a lack of respect for myself. Losing respect for yourself is a dangerous thing because, when it happens, you lose respect for others. And, from there, it's just a downward spiral. One of the biggest problems is that, as you are going down, you step on others to push yourself higher.

Failures in life and business are terrible and challenging experiences. However, the positive thing is that they provide you with a reason and an opportunity to learn. Often, when things are going well, you don't have any reason to look at what you are doing or how you are doing it. Once you have a reason to learn, you need to be willing to analyse both what went wrong and your own role in it. Based on my own experiences, I would say that you shouldn't be afraid to fail, but you have to be prepared learn from those experiences. If you learn from them, you've a better chance of going on and doing bigger and better things.

What do you look for in those you work with?

For me, ensuring that we have the right people in place is a very big part of being a good leader. I do think that there is often an under-emphasis on front-line staff in organisations. Once there are good people at the top, there can be a tendency for organisations not to worry too much about the lower level. In fact, I put far more emphasis on the people who are at the coalface and dealing with my members; they are the people who ultimately ensure that you provide a good service.

For example, among the most important people in every one of our clubs are the people working on the reception desk. They are our ambassadors. They are the first people in the organisation that our current and potential members meet. That means that I place as much importance on those staff as I do on the people who work with me on a daily basis. More specifically, although I look for quite a lot of things in people, the two most important things that I look for are personality and commitment. Once people are in a role, I also look to see whether they are getting job satisfaction. That affects how well somebody does their role and the impression they give to our members when they interact with them. Finally, I look for people who will have two-way conversations with others from all levels in the business. I look for that because I truly believe that the closer you get to the shop floor and the customer, the better the results for the organisation. If you want to get good information, you have got to have good people.

What, in your opinion, are the characteristics of effective leaders?

Nobody starts off life as a leader. You become a leader. That happens either through inheriting a formal leadership role or working your way up to earn one. I think that inheriting a leadership position is the worst possible way you can do it. It doesn't always give you the opportunity to earn the points and credibility you need to be effective. In my own life and career I have always earned the points to get the role. I suppose that's the way I like doing it, and that's the only way I think it should be done. I don't think opportunities should be handed to you on a plate. So, each time I made it to a leadership role, I got there by earning it.

For example, I think that everybody who works here in the Ben Dunne Fitness Group would have a certain amount of respect for me, because I am committed. I am here and I work fairly long hours – although I don't work any longer than I would ask anybody else to do in the organisation. For me, to earn a leadership role you have to achieve good results, you have to build a good team, there's got to be job satisfaction, people have to be earning good wages and there has to be good communication at all levels of the organisation, so that the results can be sustained.

I do find it interesting that over the course of my career I have quite often met and identified people with the qualities required to achieve these results and to become a leader. But, in general, I have found that, no matter how smart they are, only about one in ten of those who you think really have the potential to be a top-class operator or a top-class leader actually make it. I think that is because a lot of personal characteristics are tested when you are leading. In particular, I think how you react in a crisis and under pressure are important. For example, we have fire drills in our business regularly, but we actually had a real fire recently – a small one, thankfully. Even with all of the drills that we do, some people froze when it came to the real event. From what I have seen, I think that what makes the difference between potential and performance is the capacity to keep calm under pressure. From my own experience, I know that you have to earn the points to be a leader – and to stay one.

Achieving innovation and improvement in organisations: what examples do you have from the front line?

The Ben Dunne Fitness Group is now quite successful. What has made it successful is a whole combination of things, which can be described as the 'six Ps'. In fact, I have two separate formulae – one for the organisation and one for myself. The first formula is for the business itself. Regardless of what business you are in, the product has to be right, the people have to be right, and of course the price has to be right. Those three Ps are very important: Product, People and Price. I also have another formula that helps ensure that I get the three business Ps right. These are my guiding principles in life. The second set of Ps are Patience, Prudence and Persistence. When you have enough patience and prudence, then you bring in persistence. Patience and prudence help you to develop and refine ideas, while persistence helps you to get things done. So, they're my formulae for life and business. And, truly, one is as important as the other.

How do you bring about change in organisations?

Change comes about in a two-fold way, but can basically be boiled down to everyone in the business, no matter what position they are in, pushing for the organisation to do better. If the general theme and commitment that the business should do better becomes engrained, then change comes with that. Really good change comes from all of the team – those at the top and those at the coalface.

I do think that the idea that you can bring about change by demanding it is problematic. You can do it, but on a very ad-hoc and limited basis. Saying that, 'As and from 1 January, board policy is this...' is faceless and doesn't lead to lasting change. If you want to achieve change you have two choices – you can use your power or try to persuade people. The Government tends to use the power approach and says, 'As and from tomorrow, petrol will go up by 6 cent per litre.' That is one way of doing things, but in business I would advise people that, if they have good and clear lines of communication – both formal and informal – that will help a lot. Communication is therefore a big part of my style. I also spend a lot of time walking around the fitness clubs. I normally go straight to the gym area, or, as I call it, the shop floor, and I speak to the team, the instructors and the customers. And that is important, because you learn a lot by dealing directly with the people who are dealing directly with the customers. It also means that our people also have a chance to speak to me about what is happening in the organisation – and why.

I think it is very important in any organisation for the leaders to know how difficult a job the people at the coalface have to do. In this business, we close at 6.30 p.m. on weekends and we don't open until 9.30 a.m. Now, if I was thinking purely about our members, they'd have us opening the clubs at 7.00 a.m. and closing at 10.00 p.m. on a Saturday and Sunday. Every so often, our members ask me how we have such a fantastic and friendly team of people. And I have to say that the reason they are friendly is because they enjoy their job. But, if I was to ask them to work longer hours, they'd have no life. It's a rule of employment here that you only work one weekend in three, even though we're a seven-day-a-week business. And that means that I spend more time personally going around the clubs at weekends than I would during the rest of the week. Because that's when I think they need the extra attention. The reason I take that approach is that I wouldn't like to work weekends myself.

Last year I made a decision here that we were going to close for St Patrick's Day. There were people in the meeting room who said, 'Are we right to be doing this?' I turned around and asked how many of the people in that room were going to be at work on St Patrick's Day. There were seven people at the meeting, including myself, and the other six were all going to be gone. So, that's where I think an awful lot of people who lead organisations go wrong. They listen to their customers and they implement things by popular demand. But they don't take into account the most important people in a business – the people who work for you or who are on your team. And they must be number one. They need to be number one in day-to-day operations and also when you are asking them to change. You need to think about what the change means for them and their job satisfaction. If it is going to be challenging for them, then you need to persuade them of the reasons why it's worth doing. Even if it isn't great for them, if you have always tried to treat them well and put them first, they are more likely to work with you. If you make your people your number one they'll make your customers their number one. The thing that makes an organisation perform well and improve is its people – and how they are treated.

What advice do you have for aspiring leaders?

Never forget how important your people are. Lots of managers do and I think the main reasons are that they never go down to the shop floor themselves and they lose touch with what gives their people job satisfaction. I cannot sufficiently labour the point, but how you make an organisation perform, improve and go forward is by knowing what is really required at the coalface. And that same thing is going to help you bring about change. You also need to remember that there's always going to be somebody biting at your heels. If you're a good leader, there will be people who want your job. That will happen because you will have created energy around the role and a sense that the organisation is doing exciting things. People like to be associated with that kind of energy and success. So, if there's nobody after your job, question your leadership.

CONCLUSION

LESSONS IN LEADERSHIP

In the Introduction to this book, we drew attention to the current challenges facing leaders across the public, private and voluntary sectors. In recognition of the increased personal demands associated with the complex, challenging and unpredictable times we face, we now consider the role of emotion in leadership. We turn to the theme of leadership in tough times and also consider whether and how the sectoral context of leadership affects the practice of leadership. Finally, we draw attention to key leadership insights, derived from the cumulative wisdom of our interviewees.

The role of emotion in leadership

Many of our leaders articulate the importance of achieving vision through people. This generates an underlying tension between the need for emotional detachment (to facilitate analysis) and emotional engagement with others to support them through change. Nuala O'Loan notes that people are physical, intellectual and spiritual – as well as emotional – beings. She emphasises that the whole person has to be cared for. This lesson became clear for John Lonergan in the context of the move to the new women's prison in Mountjoy. In spite of gaining a beautiful new building, staff and prisoners resisted the change, due to insecurity and fear. Many of the leaders echo the sentiment that people fear uncertainty and change. On this basis, many of the leaders emphasise the importance of planning to support people's psychological and emotional reactions to change. One strategy to achieve this is provided by Niall Saul. He emphasises that leaders need to show people that they will still be able to contribute and have relevance after the change takes place. Maurice Neligan asserts that kindness goes a long way in dealing with these, and other, issues.

Our leaders draw upon their emotions to renew and develop their visions. However, they also require the capacity for detachment to engage with the issue at hand and prioritise organisational and other needs. Nuala O'Loan refers to learning detachment to facilitate analysis: to mask, manage and postpone dealing with her own emotions in difficult situations. Interestingly, the interviews emphasise that detachment is required to facilitate evaluation, not alone of problems, but of the leaders' contributions to those problems. In particular, Niall Saul notes that many organisations lose members of their top teams during significant change processes – as the leaders find it hard to dismantle what they have built. This, of course, is necessary for renewal, regeneration and, in some cases, survival.

The need to look after others' emotions and manage their own is demanding for leaders. As a result, Niall Saul raises the issue of who looks after the leaders. He places significant value on containing the anxiety of leaders with whom he works. The benefits of such support are clear.

Overall, our leaders draw attention to their need to manage emotions in a two-fold and occasionally dichotomous manner: masking and managing their own emotions to attain personal detachment while simultaneously working to provide psychological safety and security for those with whom they work. Emotion management is a challenging dimension of leadership. Given that fear is associated with change and uncertainty, emotion management is particularly important in the current context.

Leadership in tough times

The leaders note that change is usually difficult to achieve. As a result, Danuta Gray and others emphasise the importance of having a reason to make change happen. This can come from external forces or can be created internally. However, creating urgency around the need for change is difficult when the general context is positive or when an organisation is going through a successful or growth phase. In fact, Niall Saul emphasises the 'blindness of the successful', which can lead organisations into difficulty or even failure. Many of the leaders emphasise the importance of putting the need for change in context and explaining why, even if things are currently going well, the path in place does not assure continued success. This can involve getting people to think about likely issues or challenges in the future. It can also entail showing people how changing early will provide them with more options – and greater control. Leadership can be more straightforward in tough times, when the imperative for change is clear. This makes it easier for people to engage, as they often have vested interests in finding and implementing solutions.

Does context matter?

At the outset of this book we wondered whether the dynamic of leadership would be significantly affected by the sectoral context. Our leaders emphasise a common cadre of leadership activities. However, there are differences in the strategies adopted to achieve change. These predominantly stem from differences in stakeholder groups. Private sector organisations require the support of their boards, senior management and staff to achieve change. However, voluntary and public sector organisations have broader and more complex stakeholder groups. In the health sector, effective leaders are required to manage cross-professional relationships and the medical-management interface. In the public sector more broadly, leaders have to deal with transitory formal leaders in the form of politicians, as well as bureaucrats and journalists. Public sector leaders are also constrained in service development and change. They are limited by the available resources and the public policy focus.

Common strategies to achieve change

Across sectors, the leaders emphasise the need to create a reason for change and to gain support for the vision in place. Many of the leaders emphasise the importance of including staff in the construction of the vision, where feasible. This allows staff to understand and buy-in to change. It is also important as people at the coalface often have significant insights into the problems facing an organisation – and potential solutions. Ben Dunne goes walkabout in his clubs. Talking to his staff and customers gives him insight into how things are going, and provides an opportunity for staff to speak to him about the nature of, and reason for, developments in his organisation.

Niall Saul notes that getting a shared view on the threats and opportunities facing the organisation is a relatively standard component of leadership. However, the balance between analysis and action can be difficult to achieve.

Once a change is agreed, Danuta Gray emphasises the need for leaders to clearly and strongly communicate the reason for, and direction of, this change. This should preferably be done repeatedly and in a face-to-face scenario. Similarly, Nickey Brennan emphasises the need to sell the vision. For Danuta Gray, this entails being able to describe the change in a way that is relevant to the individual or group at hand. Finding a purpose that people can support or align themselves with underpins this, as many of the leaders note that people come to work to do a good job: 'If you can articulate change in the context of your key objectives, then it doesn't take a huge amount of persuasion to get people to go with you' (Danuta Gray).

Niall Saul emphasises the importance of having a small core group of people who support the change. This group should have sufficient experience to manage any likely challenges. However, their key contribution is to provide ongoing momentum.

Voluntary sector strategies to achieve change

The voluntary sector leaders stress the importance of constructively engaging with Government and other stakeholders. Nickey Brennan emphasises the importance of positioning the organisation and its contribution, relative to social and policy concerns. For example, he emphasises the broader benefits of the GAA, positioning the organisation as a social and cultural as well as a sporting outlet. He also focuses on the health benefits of sport, which align with government health policy. Sr Stanislaus Kennedy attempts to develop solutions to social issues of concern. She notes that 'showing a way forward is most definitely the best way to gain support and resources.' She describes this as 'announcing as well as denouncing'. This strategy provides a way for those being engaged – be they individuals, or in government or organisations – to both see and address the issue. In addition, she emphasises the benefit of identifying and acquiring champions for initiatives. Effective champions can communicate your message to a variety of audiences. Interestingly, Kenneth McDonald also asserts the importance of having multiple voices emphasising the same message. In hindsight, he notes that the strength of his message about heart failure may have been diluted as it emanated from a single source. For Sr Stan, the recruitment of champions requires illustrating the value of the cause. When the financial or other support of patrons is acquired, providing feedback on the impact of their support ensures that this is sustained.

Public sector strategies to achieve change

Change in the public sector is constrained by the availability of funding. It is also constrained by policy emphasis and political considerations, which are taken into account in distributing scarce resources. In acquiring such resources, Maurice Neligan emphasises the importance of generating an evidence-based case and establishing that a need exists. He emphasises liaising with those in political power to encourage them to address the issue. Interestingly, he suggests that, should support not be forthcoming, there may be an ethical imperative to inform and attain public support, using the media. Personal integrity is emphasised as a good starting point for such persuasion.

In working towards policy change, Brian Maurer stresses the need for consensus among those directly and indirectly involved, and those responsible for implementing the change. Crucially, he emphasises that funding requests presented to authorities should be agreed by all parties within the area – be that within or across institutions. Dissenting voices and competing requests for funding undermine clarity and unity of purpose.

For John Lonergan, in the absence of opportunities to effect significant change, the focus turns to maintaining services using existing resources. He notes that it is necessary not to become frustrated, as this interferes with one's capacity to achieve the optimum outcome in the particular circumstances. He also emphasises that significant resources and state-of-the-art buildings are not required to make a difference: small-scale activities, grounded in humanity and respect, can have a significant impact.

For Mark Rowe, emphasising the positive is important. Much goes right in healthcare – and in the broader public sector context. Accentuating the positive can increase momentum and provide a constructive context for change. This can be consolidated by celebrating and building upon small successes. Similarly, he notes that undertaking change on a three-month or trial basis makes it less threatening.

Delivery of change

Although many of the leaders focus their discussions on the early phases of change (getting the vision in place and securing support for this), they also emphasise the systems and processes which underpin change. Management, as well as leadership, is required for change to be implemented. In particular, Nickey Brennan emphasises the importance of systems and finance to ensure that the change is feasible and can be delivered. Nuala O'Loan emphasises the importance of quality assurance mechanisms and processes to check what is taking place. She emphasises that this is particularly important as, even if people support a change initiative, change can have unintended and unanticipated consequences. These can necessitate amendments to the original project plan.

The leaders emphasise that it is important to celebrate the small and larger successes associated with change. For Nuala O'Loan, her organisation's annual review ended in a celebration. Recognition is important: not alone for the achievement of change, but for its sustainability.

In addition to the sectoral context, further contextual influences on effective leadership were identified. In particular, attention was brought to the broader societal context (i.e. good and bad times) and the national cultural context in which the organisation is embedded. Danuta Gray emphasises that, although you have to modify your leadership style to suit the culture in which you are operating, 'the thing underneath it all, which is knowing where you're going, being able to communicate it, putting the right people in the right roles, that for me stays the same, regardless of where you work.' This lesson applies equally across sectoral and national contexts.

Closing thoughts: insights into leadership

Our leaders have drawn attention to the core and enduring dimensions of leadership and the contextual factors which affect them. Leadership is fundamentally about inspiring and supporting change. It is achieved with and through others. Leadership can demand courage, bravery and fortitude to address difficult situations and the emotions which accompany them. Crucially, with regard to our current context, the leaders have emphasised that tough times present opportunities. The current climate provides leaders with a significant platform for change. However, leaders will need a clear vision around which to mobilise support. In addition, we have seen how personal and organisational adversity has shaped the development of our leaders. The current context provides an opportunity, not alone to envision and achieve a better future, but to develop current and future leaders to secure it.